STATES' VIEW OF HEALTH CARE REFORM

THURSDAY, FEBRUARY 3, 1994

U.S. SENATE,
COMMITTEE ON FINANCE,
Washington, DC.

The hearing was convened, pursuant to notice, at 10:00 a.m., in room SD–215, Dirksen Senate Office Building, Hon. Daniel Patrick Moynihan (chairman of the committee) presiding.

Present: Senators Baucus, Mitchell, Pryor, Riegle, Rockefeller, Daschle, Breaux, Packwood, Dole, Roth, Chafee, Durenberger, Hatch, and Wallop.

Also present: Senator Robert E. Bennett.

[The press release announcing the hearing follows:]

[Press Release No. H–5, January 28, 1994]

FINANCE COMMITTEE SETS HEARING ON STATES' VIEW OF HEALTH REFORM; FOUR GOVERNORS TO TESTIFY

WASHINGTON, DC—Senator Daniel Patrick Moynihan (D–NY), Chairman of the Senate Committee on Finance, announced today that the Committee will continue its examination of health care issues with a hearing on the states' perspectives on health care reform.

The Committee will hear testimony from Gov. Carroll A. Campbell, Jr. (R–SC), Chairman of the National Governors Association, and from Gov. Howard Dean (D–VT), Gov. Lawton Chiles (D–FL) and Gov. Mike Leavitt (R–UT).

The hearing will begin at *10:00 a.m. on Thursday, February 3, 1994* in room SD–215 of the Dirksen Senate Office Building.

"Health care reform proposals before Congress would impose significant responsibilities on the states," Senator Moynihan said in announcing the hearing. "In addition, some states have experience with purchasing pools, market reforms and other important aspects of proposed national reforms. For these reasons, it is imperative that we hear the views of the National Governors Association and of individual Governors with relevant experience."

OPENING STATEMENT OF HON. DANIEL PATRICK MOYNIHAN, A U.S. SENATOR FROM NEW YORK, CHAIRMAN, COMMITTEE ON FINANCE

The CHAIRMAN. A very good morning to our guests, our distinguished witnesses. I remarked on Tuesday that the Governor's conference seemed to have accomplished more in 2 days in Washington than we have managed to do in the last year and a half or thereabouts. We are here to learn more about those views and that accomplishment.

First, as a very special honor we have Governor Leavitt of Utah; and Senator Hatch, who has to be at a meeting of the Judiciary Committee, I believe, would like to introduce his friend and Governor.

OPENING STATEMENT OF HON. ORRIN G. HATCH, A U.S. SENATOR FROM UTAH

Senator HATCH. Well, thank you, Mr. Chairman, for this courtesy because I do have to go to Judiciary where we have a markup plus a very important hearing and I just have to be there as the ranking member.

But I could not let this opportunity pass without stopping to introduce my friend, the Governor of the State of Utah, who is an expert on health care reform and really an outstanding witness as well.

Mr. Chairman, the role of the States in health care reform is one of the most fundamental issues we will consider this year. If you happen to share my belief that there is not a one-size-fits-all answer to the problems this country is experiencing with health care, what the States are considering in the way of reform becomes all the more important. And each initiative, whether it is from South Carolina, Vermont, Utah or Florida or any other State will yield valuable information on a range of issues.

I compliment you for the panel of Governors that you have here today to testify because they are excellent people. Each of them will have some perspectives that I think will add to our debate here in the Senate and to our work here.

After assuming office 1 year ago, Governor Leavitt commenced a top to bottom review of health care in Utah. The State's extensive analysis—and I might add a very healthy debate—formed the basis of Governor Leavitt's blueprint for market-oriented health care, which I believe he will discuss with the committee today.

Mike has served at all levels of government and he is a former insurance executive, so he really knows what he is talking about here. In fact, Mr. Chairman, when Mike Leavitt talks about adverse selection we will really know what adversity is.

Of course, Governor Leavitt is also appearing before the committee today as a representative of the National Governors' Association and the Health Care Leadership Group. Now we Utahans are delighted to have Mike Leavitt as our Governor. We are honored that the committee has recognized his considerable talents as well as the Governors.

I know that Governor Leavitt and all the other witnesses—Governor Campbell, Governor Dean and Governor Chiles—will provide the committee with a very beneficial perspective, which is critical to our considerations.

So I introduce to you a very dear friend of mine, one person who I have a lot of confidence in in many ways, but especially in this particular area. I hope that the committee will, as I know they will, will listen carefully and it will help us along this very important process of health care reform and the total debate that is involved.

So I want to thank you for coming, Mike.

I want to thank you, Mr. Chairman, and Senator Packwood and other members of this committee for having our Governor here.

The CHAIRMAN. We wish to thank you, Senator Hatch. We are aware that you have to be at the Judiciary Committee where you are the ranking member and you have some responsibilities this morning. We appreciate you taking this time.

S. HRG. 103–702

STATES' VIEW OF HEALTH CARE REFORM

HEARING

BEFORE THE

COMMITTEE ON FINANCE
UNITED STATES SENATE

ONE HUNDRED THIRD CONGRESS

SECOND SESSION

FEBRUARY 3, 1994

Printed for the use of the Committee on Finance

U.S. GOVERNMENT PRINTING OFFICE

81–991—CC WASHINGTON : 1994

For sale by the U.S. Government Printing Office
Superintendent of Documents, Congressional Sales Office, Washington, DC 20402
ISBN 0-16-044861-1

CONTENTS

OPENING STATEMENTS

COMMITTEE PRESS RELEASE

PUBLIC WITNESSES

ALPHABETICAL LISTING AND APPENDIX MATERIAL SUBMITTED

Governor Leavitt, we welcome you the more so because of the way you have been introduced.

Senator Packwood?

OPENING STATEMENT OF HON. BOB PACKWOOD, A U.S. SENATOR FROM OREGON

Senator PACKWOOD. Well, Mr. Chairman, this is a most interesting hearing. Tuesday was an interesting hearing. It was a stunning hearing. I am looking forward to hearing from the Governors today for a slightly different reason.

First, I take some pride in the fact that my State of Oregon last Tuesday put into effect their Medicaid plan, for which we needed a waiver from the Federal Medicaid laws. As of Tuesday, we brought 120,000 new people who had previously not been covered by Medicaid under it, but with a new system that would not have been possible without a waiver.

Here we are now talking about a national health plan and the question arises, therefore, can you have a national health plan if you have State variances. And if your answer is no, then Oregon would not have gotten its waiver.

If you say, well, yes, then the question becomes, how far can you allow the waivers before you no longer have a national health plan and what Lawton Chiles wants to try in Florida may be different than what other Governors want to try elsewhere; and maybe what he wants to try in Florida fits Florida and does not fit South Dakota.

Do you allow those kind of variances? What do you do about ERISA? Whereby, those employers who are national say that it is not fair to them that they have to meet different standards in different States which confuses and makes impossible any kind of uniform company-wide, nationwide health plan, and it is an understandable argument, unless they are exempt from State variances.

And if enough of them are exempt, then the State cannot put a plan into effect very well because too many people in it are simply exempt. Those are legitimate questions that are part of a problem of a Federal system.

So I look forward very much to the Governors' comments on this. I will say again, without variance, Oregon would not be able to try what it is so proud of starting to try last Tuesday.

Thank you.

The CHAIRMAN. Thank you, sir. I would just comment that we agreed in our last meeting that we would withhold our opening statements, beyond just welcoming our guests, until the questioning began.

Governor Campbell is just a little bit behind schedule this morning. He probably is at the White House this very moment. So we will proceed.

We also have with us Governor Chiles, our old friend and dear friend and colleague.

Governor Dean, you come as the Vice Chairman, you are after Governor Campbell and, of course, you are Dr. Dean. So you are doubly welcome. Would you proceed, sir. Take all the time you want. We have all the time you may require.

STATEMENT OF HON. HOWARD DEAN, GOVERNOR OF THE STATE OF VERMONT AND VICE CHAIRMAN, NATIONAL GOVERNORS' ASSOCIATION

Governor DEAN. Thank you very much, Senator, and thank you for your gracious appearance before us last weekend when we were here. I have prefiled testimony. I am going to be very brief.

The CHAIRMAN. We will put all testimony in the record as if read, and you proceed just as you choose.

Governor DEAN. Good. I will proceed briefly so that we can hear from all the Governors and have a question period, because I am sure there will be a lot of good interchange, there.

I am going to talk about what is going on in Vermont. Governor Campbell when he gets here——

The CHAIRMAN. Could I just say Governor Campbell has arrived. We were aware that you were running just a little bit behind. So we have asked Governor Dean to begin and he has just done so.

Governor CAMPBELL. Please let him go ahead, Senator, in the interest of time and then I will be glad to say whatever you would like, sir.

The CHAIRMAN. Thank you.

Governor DEAN. I will be very quick. Governor Campbell will go through the National Governors position on health care reform. I just want to say that I am very grateful to Governor Campbell for his flexibility and leadership. We think we have made some significant progress, at least among Governors, in understanding there will be compromises made in the long run. There are some things that Governor Campbell and his party do not like in this bill, which we understand and want to be flexible about. There are probably things that he does not like in the bill that we hope he will move a little bit our way on. We were very encouraged by some of the discussions we had this week.

Governor Campbell will talk about the NGA policy. I am going to talk a little bit about what we hope we will be doing in Vermont and what we have done in Vermont and how that fits in with the President's plan and with other plans you might consider.

We understand that we cannot have 50 different State solutions to the health care crisis. But we do need some flexibility. Delivering care in New York is different than delivering care certainly in Vermont or South Carolina. Each State needs some freedom and flexibility to design their own programs, specifically with the ERISA waiver, which we, of course, are very much in favor of.

We understand the need to be able to do business in all 50 States. We believe that the waiver could be very narrowly crafted to apply to health care and still have enough flexibility so that Oregon could do what Oregon needed to do without upsetting the plans of the multi-national corporations.

In 1991, the Vermont legislature adopted a community rating and guaranteed acceptance for the small group market. We banned pre-existing condition exclusions for that market and we were the first State in the country to do that. A number of insurers said all sorts of dreadful things would happen and there were some folks who moved out of the State, some small insurers. Frankly, I think that was to the benefit of both the rate payers and the people of the State.

The next year we understood that if we did not do the same thing in the individual market that many employers could simply get around reforms by kicking their people out of group plans and into the individual plans. So we had individual reform and applied the same standards.

There are some rate bans. But basically we have community rating for everybody in Vermont, both group and individual. And there has been no rate shock. In fact, we think it has improved the premium situation, particularly for the larger businesses where there is a lot of cost shifting going on.

In 1992 in addition to reforming the individual mandate we did some tort reform. We the National Governors, hope very much, that the Congress will give us some broad outlines for national tort reform. But we did some of that which we think will work for Vermont. It may not do for some of the larger States like New York or California.

Our tort reform essentially requires that all disputes be submitted to an arbitrator. They cannot go directly to court. And if they do proceed to court after that, the verdict of the Arbitration Board is admissible as evidence.

We think that may do in Vermont. Again, perhaps not in other States. The Governors urge the Federal Government to set some broad guidelines on tort reform and to enact some of that, as well.

We expanded our Medicaid program so that all children in Vermont have health insurance. Essentially, we guarantee coverage to everybody at 225 percent of poverty or below 18 years of age or younger felt that was a down payment on what we hoped would be our universal program.

We also set up a global budgeting process, which became voluntary last July 1st and becomes mandatory on this July 1st so that we have the right to control all health care expenditures in the State. We did it voluntarily for a year to gather the data, which obviously has been a major Federal issue as well. We think we will be ready to do the global budget, although we now have a major bill in front of us and will refine that global budget this year.

The law created the Vermont Health Care Authority which consolidated a lot of the health care regulatory apparatus in the State, but it also was charged with delivering us a single-payer model and a regulated multi-payer model. The report came out in November.

Shortly after that, we, based on their report, introduced a multi-payer regulated model which looks somewhat like the President's plan.

Individuals under our plan—individuals and employers—would be required to pay for coverage. There is an employer mandate in our plan. However, the mandate is 50 percent, not 80 percent. The reason that I did that is because I told the business community that they would have a major say in how this was going to be financed, but we needed to do it. We needed to get everybody covered and we had to get costs under control. But I would leave to them how that could be financed because they were the ones that were going to pay most of the money.

I heard very early on that a payroll tax was not something the business community wanted us to do. There were a lot of good arguments for a payroll tax. It was more equitable, fairer to small businesses.

An employer mandate was, therefore, the only other possibility, other than a very large general fund tax increase, which was not supported by very many people at all.

The 50 percent premium works much better for the business community in Vermont because we have a great many small businesses. About half the businesses under 10 employees, of which there are 9,000 in our State, give health insurance; and most of them give health insurance at 50 percent or slightly above, not at 80 percent the larger employers are.

So by coming in at a 50 percent mandate we essentially took all those folks out of the problem. They no longer have a problem. In fact, I think many of them like it because they understand that it is going to even things out between themselves and their competitors who do not give health insurance at all.

We also are expanding Medicaid because we do not have the luxury of Federal help with this to cover adults up to 100 percent of poverty. Expanding Medicaid will take some of the very low income people who are working and put them under help, and also expand the coverage to children to 300 percent of poverty. Families who make an income of $43,000 or less will—at least their kids—will be automatically guaranteed health care.

We will have to increase our payments for Medicaid because we understand that what we have done may put in jeopardy some of the small rural physician practices and we do not want that to happen.

There are no employer subsidies. We have gone down to 50 percent. But there is a hidden subsidy in that we are now taking over many of the responsibilities for their dependents and for individuals up to 100 percent of Medicaid. So in essence we are going to be largely responsible for the costs of some of the employees that now would have to be paid for entirely.

We do have an employee subsidy. We start at 300 percent of poverty and the subsidy grows as you get down towards 150 or 100 percent. I, frankly, cannot remember if it is at 150 or 100 where we totally subsidize. I suspect it is 100. So we ask the employees to contribute more and more as their income rises. Over 300 percent of poverty, they are expected to pick up the entire 50 percent.

There is also a fund available, as there was in Hawaii, when they went to an employer mandate for businesses, that can be used if businesses can show us that this would put them out of business. In Hawaii they only used about $80,000 worth of that fund in 20 years. So we are prepared to help them out, but we are not expecting a large deluge.

There are others. We have multiple alliances. We have a State-run alliance, which would cover all Medicaid recipients. Medicare recipients very badly want to be in our program. We cannot afford to do that without help from the Federal Government, because our benefit package, while it is certainly not a Cadillac it is probably a reasonably well equipped Chevrolet.

It is our State employees benefit package. We have no first-dollar coverage in our State employees benefit package. But we are adding some for immunizations and well-child visits and pap smears and the kind of thing that is ultimately going to save us money. We want no barriers to that.

We have beefed up the mental health a little. I think the status of mental health insurance in this country is pretty appalling. So we have tried to put that at parity. But other than that, it is basically the State employees package, which is a decent package but certainly nothing extravagant.

The alliances would cover the State employees, would cover perhaps other public employees, would cover Medicaid. Ultimately we will ask for a waiver if this passes and put Medicare in there, although we will need some Federal help to bring their package up to what the State package is, principally the addition of prescriptions. Of course, we understand that they will have to continue to pay as well.

In our bill we have alliances so the private sector may go into their alliances if they wish. There is a transition period for a 2-year period, where they do not have to join after 2 years in our proposal. Now they do have to join. Obviously, we have a Republican Senate and a Democratic House. We suspect there will be some compromise in that issue as we move along.

But we very much want to encourage the private sector to continue doing all the things they have done so far to control costs.

There are those, of course, in the legislature that would like to pay for all of this with tax money and so forth and so on and there is a wide spectrum of opinion just as you have here. I cannot predict what is going to come out, but we believe we are in the middle of a political spectrum and that our approach is reasonable and fair and satisfactory.

There are some tax increases required. They are not extravagant. We are going to do this mostly on splinter taxes. Obviously, if we were to do away with the mandate that would be a source of funding that we would not have and we would have to make up more of that with general tax revenue. I think that is a compromise that will certainly be discussed.

There are those who would like to go to 80 percent. I believe that would be tougher on small businesses without the kind of subsidies that the President talks about, which we cannot afford at the State level.

There are those who would like to have no mandate, and obviously then we have to raise more taxes and have higher user costs. I think those are on the other end more difficult.

The one thing that I would like to say, and I am sure that Governor Campbell is going to say this in our policy, is that we really desperately feel you need to enact something this year.

The only criticism I have of the Clinton bill, although we are certainly willing to understand other people's criticism and willing to be flexible about it, the only criticism that I have personally is that it does not let us go fast enough. Our bill calls for enactment of universal access on January 1, 1995. Everybody would be covered and all this would be in effect.

The Clinton bill, the earliest we could go is 1996. We would like the ability to go when we are ready to go. We understand and we support the Governors position that we want to have a national benefits package.

Senator PACKWOOD. Did you say universal access or universal coverage?

Governor DEAN. Both.

Senator PACKWOOD. Both.

Governor DEAN. To me the terms are indistinguishable.

Senator PACKWOOD. All right.

Governor DEAN. We spent a lot of time arguing about that this weekend.

The CHAIRMAN. We spend a lot of time on semantics around here.

Governor DEAN. Yes.

The CHAIRMAN. But I think we have agreed to distinguish between universal coverage and universal access. I think that is an important point.

Governor DEAN. Well, we spent a lot of time trying to distinguish and I think our conclusion was that we did not do such a good job trying to distinguish that.

The CHAIRMAN. When you use a word it means exactly what you mean it to be.

Governor DEAN. I use the word access to mean that everybody has health care available to them, which means financially available as well as available in terms of a rural problem or appropriate health care where it is needed.

The CHAIRMAN. Fine.

Governor DEAN. So just to conclude, I know Florida has made a lot of progress, Washington State, other places are moving right along, Minnesota another one, and others have made a tremendous amount of progress.

Hawaii, obviously, dealt with their situation. Although as Senator Dole pointed out earlier in the week, they have not gotten there entirely either.

I strongly believe we need a national framework for this. The sooner it happens, the better. My own personal opinion is that we have looked at the Breaux bill, the President's bill, and the Chafee bill, and there are a lot of good things we like in all of them. There are some things we very much dislike in them.

But I think, if you look at all those three bills, they are not so very far apart that pieces of those could be fashioned to making something that probably everybody at this table could live with. We wish you well and we want to be as helpful as we can in helping you to get there.

The CHAIRMAN. We thank you, Doctor. We certainly need all the well wishing we can get.

The CHAIRMAN. Senator Dole has not had a chance to make an opening statement in this series. But I gather you would rather wait to hear from Governor Campbell.

Senator DOLE. I have made enough statements recently. [Laughter.]

The CHAIRMAN. Thank you, Dr. Dean.

Governor Campbell, sir, we welcome you to present the Governors' views on this subject.

STATEMENT OF HON. CARROLL A. CAMPBELL, JR., GOVERNOR OF THE STATE OF SOUTH CAROLINA, AND CHAIRMAN, NATIONAL GOVERNORS' ASSOCIATION

Governor CAMPBELL. Thank you, Mr. Chairman. I am glad to be here and we appreciate this opportunity to come before the committee.

The National Governors' Association has come together in a very unusual time—that is, when this debate is raging around Capitol Hill and the country—we reached a consensus which is often difficult to do. We have these items that we wanted to give you.

I will speak as Chairman of the National Governors' Association in giving the Governors' position. And at such time that I am asked on any other particular point I will try and differentiate and tell you when it is personal and when it is a policy position.

The CHAIRMAN. Fine.

Governor CAMPBELL. But you have our written statement and I am not going to read it. I just want to make a few points.

As you know, the Governors just completed our midwinter meeting where we adopted what I believe is an important framework for reform. We realize that despite our differences on employer mandates and global budgets and mandatory alliances that there is a great deal of common ground among all of us about strategies to address the nation's health care problems. There was also a strong belief that these reforms should be undertaken, if at all possible, this year.

Mr. Chairman, I am not trying to say there is total unanimity among the Governors. But we did have enough to pass policy. The policy that did pass was passed unanimously by the Governors that were present at that time, which was a large group.

Some would go a lot further than we have gone in our policy and some think it has gone too far. But we became convinced that we could contribute most to the national debate by adopting a policy which reflects the consensus that we have.

These are the things it includes: insurance reform to ensure portability of coverage; state authorized purchasing cooperatives, but does not specify mandatory or voluntary; a core benefits package that will be offered, but not necessarily paid for by employers; a cap on tax deductibility that is the same for everybody, scaled of course to cost of region and inflation—even though we have not specified that, that has been generally our understanding; subsidies for low income individuals who cannot afford insurance; flexibility to move the current Medicaid population to managed care settings; malpractice reform and antitrust relief; federally organized outcome and quality standards and administrative simplifications; and the ability for States to get ERISA waivers.

We hope that as you go forward, Mr. Chairman, and members of the committee, that you will keep this framework in mind and the Governors' position that it is imperative to get Federal action on these issues at the earliest possible date.

I know that you asked the NGA to respond to a number of specific questions and these are addressed in the written statement which you have before you. However, I would like to comment briefly on just a couple of them.

You asked about the extent to which Federal reform should seek to even out spending among States. Mr. Chairman, I know that the Medicaid formula is a particularly contentious question for you and the State of New York, but it has traditionally been the role of the Federal Government to assist the disadvantaged and that is the root of the disparities in the Medicaid matching rate, which is based largely on income.

As far as so-called low effort States, the Southern States might lag behind in raw dollars spent per person on Medicaid, but as a percentage of their budgets the southern States generally spend more on Medicaid than their northern counterparts—16.8 percent versus 15.4 percent of the budgets.

In my own State we also invest a great deal in the public health side of health care because that is a big provider, especially in our rural areas.

I am going to deviate from my testimony and just say something on the word "access." If we are talking about insurance, you can use the term that you have access to insurance. But if I give you insurance and there is nobody there within 50 to 75 miles to give you care, it is not worth a whole lot. Access also means access to somebody that can deliver the service. And availability might mean availability of insurance or service.

But I think it is extremely important for us to recognize that the infrastructure does not exist in this country just to give everybody insurance and say that we have gotten them health care because they cannot get to it. So that is something that we in some of our States with more rural populations understand because we have to operate a major public effort to get out to these areas.

Senator RIEGLE. Mr. Chairman, could I just ask one question at this point?

The CHAIRMAN. You surely can. Yes, sir.

Senator RIEGLE. I appreciate the point you are making. This is a very important discussion. I would like to relate your point to what Governor Dean said a minute ago.

He defines access as meaning that you can both get the insurance and afford to pay for it, whatever the scheme is. And you make the further distinction that you may have the insurance but if there is nobody out there providing the service you are still left short. I think that is an equally important point.

Do you agree with his point that access means it has to be affordable? In other words, it may be available to everybody but that does not mean anything if you cannot afford to pay for it. Are you two in agreement on that point as well?

Governor CAMPBELL. For low income people we think there has to be a subsidy. We have it now in Medicaid and we think it has to be in some other areas. The availability for people that could pay for it, should fall on the people that can pay for it and not the taxpayers to pay for it.

Senator RIEGLE. I will just prolong this one more minute.

Governor CAMPBELL. Sure.

Senator RIEGLE. Because it is so critical to the whole way we fashion this thing. We now define certain people as being low income and so we help them. We subsidize them with Medicaid. But there is the instance of people who are the working poor, who are a notch above Medicaid. Some people do not want to get off welfare because they do not want to lose their health care, which they cannot afford if they go up a notch on the economic ladder.

If you come out of the Medicaid population and look to the next tier of people who are the working poor, is there a consensus among the Governors as to how we solve the affordability and, therefore, the access problem for that group. Health care no matter how you do it is expensive. There is no way to get it for free.

So what is the view on how we handle that tier of people which unfortunately is a pretty good sized tier in our country?

Governor CAMPBELL. There are different views on this. But let me be very specific about one view, that happens to be my own. I have a demonstration grant program going on in a part of my State right now which allows employers that have low income employees to buy into our Medicaid plan with a co-payment. That accesses the system for them. It works. It is just on a test basis.

But these are the kinds of things that do work because you do have to bridge that gap. But we are asking that there be a co-payment to offset the cost of doing this.

This whole thing is driven by cost. I think we all need to understand that. We can design every plan in the world if we can pay for it.

There is another thing that we are doing in our State. We have a waiver that is pending, that we are working with the administration on which would put our Medicaid program under managed care.

Medicaid is one of the reasons that we are running up the costs of insurance and health care in this country today. It is the most expensive system in the world. It is mostly after-the-fact medicine. If we manage this care we can affect some savings.

Disproportionate share payments into our hospitals now pays for serving the poor, serving those people that you are talking about that do not have anywhere to go. So they go to the hospital, and are in the system in the most expensive way.

We believe in our State that we can effect savings and expand access by putting Medicaid under managed care with primary care physicians and a primary care network—and let me tell you, the network is important. Because in order to provide real access I have to use health departments, nurse practitioners, and physician extenders as well as hospitals and physicians. So we have to build the networks in order to get there.

But we believe putting the Medicaid into a managed care network will effect some savings. And at the same time we want to take some of the disproportionate share payments to hospitals and expand Medicaid eligibility to people that are up to 100 percent of the poverty level, the working poor. You have to do it in steps to pay for it.

So there will be different ideas on how to do it. But we are going to have to address the problem. Our idea is to utilize what we have, try to get it under control, and then get to it. But I agree with your point.

Senator RIEGLE. Thank you, Mr. Chairman.

Governor CAMPBELL. I am sure that Congress is going to look at these formulations in equity, Mr. Chairman, that we talked about;

and I am sure you will take the fact as I mentioned earlier into account.

But you also asked about the willingness of States to be accountable for health care expenditures in partnership with the Federal Government. It is an impossible question to answer with any degree of specificity at this stage in the debate since we do not know what kind of reform we are eventually looking at.

We would have to understand what kind of details. We certainly would have to say this, that we understand that we will have to uphold our side of a partnership. The States do not want to be accountable for budgets and budget overruns without having control of a system or the ability to take actions to cut costs.

Howard said he put in a global budget in his State. He can control that through his legislature for his State expenditures. If the global budget is controlled in Washington, I do not have much control over it in South Carolina when it is squeezed down and we have to keep on giving the services.

So there is a difference between us having some ability where we can handle it or having the controls at another level of government. So that is our concern.

States are deeply concerned about the tendency of members on both sides of the aisle to finance reform with Medicaid and Medicare savings and/or caps in disproportionate share dollars. Unless we restructure, we do not think those dollars are there. You have to restructure the system and your Medicaid to get those dollars. You cannot just cap them, because Medicaid is growing.

We have to restructure in disproportionate share to get those dollars to that marginal group that we are now serving and to pick up some of those costs. So just to cap Medicaid and to claim that without having a restructuring of that group of people is not going to capture the dollars.

I am going to talk in a minute about what we are trying to do in our State on a bipartisan basis. I mentioned a few things awhile ago. But I want to say that the Governors' Association as a whole is strongly supportive of removing Federal barriers to the State-based health reform that is going on now, including Medicaid and comprehensive waivers.

ERISA exemptions and relief from the Boren Amendment are necessary if we are going to be able to do some of the things.

Our written statement addresses these issues, but I want to emphasize that Governors believe that States ought to be able to experiment with reform so long as they have the support of their legislatures and their citizens.

In a time when Congress is seriously considering blowing up the whole national system and replacing it with an untried substitute, I guess our plea is this—look at some of the things that have taken place in the States and see what works. There are things out there all across the country and I think that you can build on some experience. That is the way we ought to go at this.

Our statement also comments on the four bills before your committee from the point of view of NGA policy. I understand, Mr. Chairman, you decided to go through the process issue by issue area. And if you go through the process issue by issue rather than bill by bill, I think you will be well served in reaching a final conclusion. I compliment you on that decision.

Now, Mr. Chairman, I would like to tell the committee about how all of this National reform discussion translates into some action. I have already mentioned to you what is happening in the State. Let me give you some exact figures.

In the State of South Carolina we have not raised the premiums on our State employees for the last 3 years—3 years. We are in a PPO system which includes virtually all of our providers. State employees have a choice of doctors. It is a PPO based on fee-for-service, and it includes co-payments. Our providers have agreed to take the insurance payment and the co-payment.

When you compare our program with Medicaid, we are looking at a huge differential. Medicaid costs since the beginning of 1988 went up from $120 million to $341 million in 3 years. We have had to continually had to match up, up, up as the programs are liberalized and the money does not follow.

And yet in our employee systems we are able to handle the costs. This is what Governor Cuomo was talking about in New York—about the State employees—and they are concerned with it. This is a real concern.

In South Carolina we know that we can, by reorganizing Medicaid in disproportionate share, probably pick up 120,000 more people in our program—the marginal people we were talking about a moment ago. That is major progress.

Because then employment will be no bar to health coverage for this low income population and because it removes a disincentive to work, particularly for the current welfare population. But these linkages are essential.

Like many of my colleagues I believe we can use our Medicaid resources more efficiently and effectively. And our waiver, I hope, will do that. Each client in our program will have a medical home with a physician, as I said, or a clinic.

But we are going to emphasize something else, and that is good preventive and primary care services as well as the notions of wellness and personal responsibility. We will be able to streamline the cumbersome and expensive eligibility process not only for the State and Federal Government but for our providers as well.

We are looking to build a stronger system and we are looking to build an infrastructure. We are also attempting to answer some very tough questions about how best to provide good health care services to the special populations covered by Medicaid—the elderly, the disabled, and the people with serious and chronic mental illness—because we have to face that in this whole program.

Mr. Chairman, I understand that adequate financing and access to care is crucial to these items and I am working with our providers to ensure an adequate capitation rate to encourage doctors, hospitals and clinics to participate. We have to have the participation of the whole system to do anything long term.

I believe that what many of us are proposing will be a foundation for good public policy. The public side of health care is not the only concern for us though. With the bipartisan support of many in our State, we are proposing a package of proposals that will build on the efforts that we have made in the past.

81-991 O - 94 - 2

For instance, we concentrated first on the children by opting to cover pregnant women and children up to 185 percent of poverty under Medicaid. We also implemented a program called Caring for Tomorrow's Children. We cut our infant mortality rate by 18.5 percent in the last 3 years without putting any new money in.

I will tell you what we did. We bribed them to go to the doctor. We asked the private sector to participate by donating everything from diapers to milk to pizzas to hairdos. We then produced a coupon book. Doctors and clinics providing prenatal care validate the coupons. Every fifth coupon is good for a taxi fare so that people could get to the clinic.

We went to the television stations and got them to run public service announcements the people began to use the system the way they were supposed to use it and it began to have an impact on infant mortality.

We are also doing a statewide immunization campaign. We started out with all of the doctors, the hospitals, the public health service and everybody. Our first step was to get every child immunized before they entered day care.

Our effort now is to get every child immunized before they are 2 years of age. When we started this new effort about 4 months ago, we had 63 percent of our children immunized. We are now up to about 74 percent. We think we can hit about 82 percent by May. And our goal is to have 100 percent by May of 1995.

We have also sought to increase access by enacting legislation supporting current programs throughout the State and we will use our retired physicians as screening physicians. In many instances they are clustered and can practice part-time and do health screening for people and do some primary care service and they do it pro bono. We have put in a retired physician network to try to reach out to get some of these people. We have expanded the authority of physician assistants and nurse practitioners and others.

The reforms that we are going to be pushing will include insurance reform and antitrust reform to the extent we can do it. But I am proud of our progress in South Carolina and I am proud of what we have worked nationally on to build a consensus among the Governors.

I am equally proud of the relationship that Governor Dean and I have had. We have different beliefs on this subject, but he is a person working to find a solution. I am a person working to find a solution. And I believe that, of course, Governor Leavitt and Governor Chiles are also. We appreciate the opportunity to make a presentation, sir.

The CHAIRMAN. We thank you, Governor Campbell.

[The prepared statement of Governor Campbell appears in the appendix.]

The CHAIRMAN. Indeed, we congratulate you and Governor Dean for bringing the Governors together in such a dramatic and significant way. That list of things on which you are substantially agreed is very close to a national health care reform. Not as far as some of us would go, further than some others, but it is a very important event.

We are going to hear all of our Governors. Next is our former colleague and cherished friend, Governor Chiles of Florida.

STATEMENT OF HON. LAWTON CHILES, GOVERNOR OF THE STATE OF FLORIDA

Governor CHILES. Thank you, Mr. Chairman and members of the committee. I thank you very much for inviting me to testify today. Certainly there is no greater topic that we have than the one that you all are dealing with, and no greater problem that our country faces.

It certainly affects trying to run a State Government in every way imaginable. In 1961 when I took office our employers had experienced a premium increase of over 20 percent a year for over 10 years. And Medicaid growth of nearly 30 percent a year just shifted all of our State priorities.

We had to make drastic cuts in education, in public safety, in environment, in family support programs. And if you looked at the percentage of our revenue that we were able to contribute to education, it went from 65 percent to 50 and that happened all across the board because of this explosion that we were seeing.

Seattle in 1991 brought by a bipartisan group of Governors said we could not wait until the year 2000 to have universal access. In Florida we felt that we could not wait at all. We had to try to go forward and do as much as we possibly could do.

So in a bipartisan way in 1992 in Florida we passed the outline of a plan to set a goal for full access by December 31, 1994. That would be this year.

Then with that we were able and have passed a health reform bill every year. I would say the commitment for universal coverage was the starter or helped us bring together everything that we have been able to do. Because in effect we said we are going to do this by December 31, 1994 and we will try to do it in voluntary ways. If we cannot, we will go to a mandatory way.

That brought everybody to the table—industry, health providers, government—to say, how is the way that we can best do it. So that put the gun at our head and forced us to do something.

Last year we set up managed competition models in each of our 11 different community health purchasing alliances to give small business access to affordable health care. Those alliances will allow businesses of 1 to 50 employees guaranteed issue, modified community ratings, comparative information on health care reforms.

Our alliances have sent out requests for proposals and they will be coming in February 10. Each of those 11 alliances will be looking at bids. And it is interesting, we have roughly 100 different insurance companies, PPO's, HMO's, combinations of doctors and others that are ready to bid.

In the coming year we are going to enact reforms to extend coverages in the alliances to individuals, work to develop a long term plan to reverse the ratio of primary care to specialist practitioners, physicians and enact a comprehensive basic benefit package which will provide benefits you and I have been enjoying for a long time.

In total, you know, we have a plan with 100 detailed recommendations. We had 13 advisory groups. We held over 100 public meetings. So we tried to have a bottom-up plan. I said earlier the 1980's premiums grew by 20 percent a year. Last year our employers' premiums grew at 2 percent while the national average was over 8 percent.

So this again is before we have opened a single bid, so you see the market is responding. Hospitals have started merging; doctors have decided to get together; people are, you know—competition is happening as they structure to get forward to that.

I try to tell my business people that what that means is, Florida has a billion $100,000 premium in effect to use for capital job formation as opposed to even the national average and I think you are seeing the national average begin to respond to what is anticipated out there.

So these savings help us this year for the first time. I had rather than zero dollars because all of my new revenue had been eaten up in the AFDC and the Medicaid and the State employees and we were not able to give an employee pay raise for 3 years because we were paying the employee premiums that we are accenting this year we had additional dollars that we could put back into education, and to prevention, and to public safety, and some of those other areas without raising taxes.

I might say, we also, because we cut our Medicaid cost growth in less than half and a lot of that was in the health care cost, we were able to return to you $400 million that could be used in deficit reduction for what your share would have been of our Medicaid premium.

So Florida—like Oregon, Hawaii, Vermont, Tennessee, Utah, South Carolina, Minnesota—made strides in the last 3 years, but we have not turned the corner. I am concerned that, you know, there is a feeling to some that there is no longer a crisis in health care. They point to the progress that we have made and I point to the progress we made in Florida too, but we do not have a solution.

We made progress in cutting the growth of the premium costs that were hemorrhaging and had been hemorrhaging. We have not made progress in cutting the number of uninsured. In fact, Robert Wood Johnson in our State says the percentage of people without insurance went from 18.5 percent of our population to nearly 20 percent. That has happened over the last year. So that compares with a rate of about 15 percent nationwide.

So the tragedy of this fact is when we acknowledge that three out of four of those people that are uninsured are working people or the families of working people, the very people that we are talking about encouraging not to get on welfare or these things, these are the people that are going without coverage.

I will not burden with telling you the letters we receive every day of the people that are in that crisis because they do not have that insurance, locked into employment where they are, unable to get coverages that they have. But according to the Rand Corporation about half of our businesses do not offer coverage and that figure, I think, holds true nationally for businesses with less than 50 employees.

Our greatest challenge is with businesses with less than five employees, two-thirds of them in my State do not offer insurance. So the costs are coming down. Access is not being expanded. In fact, it is shrinking. So the restructuring of our economy again has brought us more small business. Unfortunately, these businesses are less likely to insure.

We are fortunate, I think, to have a President and a First Lady willing to face the challenge and articulate it well enough to explain this to the American people. I think the promise of having to have access and coverage for all people is just so necessary that we just have to do that if we are going to compete as a nation. Certainly my State has to have that if we are going to be able to survive.

We need the flexibility and I feel like that the President's plan now gives us basically the flexibility. I would like to go faster than that plan goes. But it allows us to address our unique problems. It, I think, gives us most importantly a realistic goal of universal coverage with some comprehensive budget.

So I return to the fact that it was the point of requiring universal coverage that we put in our first plan that we enacted that I think allowed us to make the steps of progress. Without universal coverage, all the gains that we made on the cost side will slowly or faster disappear.

So our public hospitals today estimate that cost shift on the uninsured nearly doubles the bill of the paying patients. Now without universal coverage cost shifting is going to continue and health care inflation spiral will also continue.

So our current system is a drift and universal coverage is the only anchor that I see that can study it. I used to think when I was here that when we would look at the Kennedy plan or some other plans that we could not address extended coverage until we could control cost. I now have become a convert and realize you cannot control until you have expanded coverage, until you really have universal coverage.

So we have adopted the key elements of the President's plan. We folded them into our effort to expand coverage to more than half of our uninsured by doing what South Carolina and other States are doing. We have submitted our waiver to put Medicaid into managed care and use those savings to expand our coverage.

We have it on a voluntary basis of allowing employers and employees to contribute up to 250 percent of poverty. We think that the administration will give us that waiver based on the other waivers they have granted. And when we do that, we will have covered about half of our uninsured. I know of no way we can go further without a national plan, without help from the Federal Government, or without mandates that we would have to try and enact in Florida if something does not happen here.

I think once we get there and we will have—you know, we already have reduced our costs, we already have made the burden less on any business or any individuals that are out there, but once you reach that point, if we do not close that loop, I see it all starting to unravel, at least we will not have a problem.

So first just to say a couple of myths on mandates or on these things, I do not think any State like Florida can provide universal coverage and reform the health care system by itself. We just cannot do it. Without your leadership and your attention and direction, we cannot go much further than we have attempted to go now.

Second, as bold as our solution is, we can only reduce our uninsured by about half. That is still going to leave us with over a million people over 10 to 12 percent of our population that will not have coverage.

And third, while we will not reform the system overnight, I do not think we can approach it in a timid incremental approach. Again, without our goal of December of 1994, we could not have moved where we did.

So I urge you this year to go as far and do as much as you possibly can. And finally, I think we have to recognize that the most affordable system is not going to attract all comers. That is the primary deficiency of a totally voluntary system, is that those who choose not to buy are the ones that the rest of us have to pay for. And as long as that happens, we again will have this spiral of cost that we cannot control.

In our own State we have great hopes for our reform and the affect we will have in closing that gap as much as we can. But I think now we need the partnership. It needs to be done in a bipartisan way. We understand that.

I am delighted to see that there is a Breaux bill and that there is a John Chafee bill and there is the President's bill. I urge you as you put those bills together, make sure you do close the loop. Because if you do not close the loop and get us universal coverage, we will not be able to have our people insured in Florida.

The CHAIRMAN. We thank you, Governor.

[The prepared statement of Governor Chiles appears in the appendix.]

The CHAIRMAN. May I just take the point of personal privilege you might say to note that sentence in your third paragraph which you did not read in your text which said, "Franklin Roosevelt once said that 'practically all the things we have done in the Federal Government are like things Al Smith did as Governor of New York'"—underscoring that many of the new social programs, including Social Security and unemployment compensation, were modeled on successful State programs.

I think we have been hearing this and there is a lot for us to learn. I think we are in that process.

And so finally we turn to Governor Leavitt who was introduced earlier by our colleague, Senator Hatch. Good morning, Governor. Would you proceed, sir?

STATEMENT OF HON. MICHAEL O. LEAVITT, GOVERNOR OF THE STATE OF UTAH

Governor LEAVITT. Good morning, Senator. I am delighted to be here. May I just say that today I will focus on one basic thought. I submitted my written testimony. I think that we are in this boat together. I do not believe that there is a way that States, as good as the plans that you have heard detailed today, are going to be able to solve this problem on our own.

On the other hand, I would submit to you that I do not suspect it is going to be done well without us.

I am here today really to plead the case that States right now who are moving forward need three things. We need some tools. We need some time tables. And we need some flexible frameworks upon which to work.

Let me just briefly tell you a little bit about our process. We call it the Utah Health Print. May I suggest in summary that if you were to take the NGA policy position and lay it on top of this you would basically have the NGA policy position embodied in a plan.

This came independently. It is somewhat coincidental. But I think it may in fact mean there is some good sense in the NGA policy position.

We had to make some basic decisions, like all States and like you will. We had first of all to make a decision as to whether we thought having health insurance was an individual responsibility or whether it needed to become a business responsibility or the government's responsibility.

In our State, we have opted to keep it an individual responsibility. Our plan does not contemplate any employer mandates. However, it does call in 1998 if we are not successful at what we are doing we have to revisit that question.

Second, we had to determine whether or not we wanted to fix the market place or whether we wanted to go back and have a government run program. It did not take us long to figure what we wanted. We did not want government run health care. In our State we would like to have the marketplace define it.

Third, and I think a very important one, was a question of whether or not this was an event or, in fact, whether or not this was a process. We have opted for a process because we do not believe it can be done at one time.

Our Health Print includes seven steps, seven annual benchmarks or seven annual—we call them decision windows. Now we have the disadvantage or some would call an advantage in our State of only having our legislature in session for 45 days each year.

So we not only have to deal with 700-some odd pieces of legislation, and a budget, but we are also trying to deal with pieces of health care legislation during this 45-day session.

But we think that is, in fact, an advantage. So we broke it into seven different pieces, starting this year, taking a very large step in being able to meet those.

The fourth one was how much choice. Now there are a lot of things we did not know in our State as a matter of certainty. One thing we have found as a matter of certainty is that the more choices folks have, the more expensive this becomes; and the fewer choices they have, the less expensive it becomes.

So we had to make a decision on where we would come down and we concluded that there was a middle ground—that is, that we would let people make choices on their own. If they were willing to pay more, they could have more choices. If they were willing to pay less, they would have fewer choices, with one very, very important exception.

That is, we concluded that if our State Government was going to be paying the bill for people that, in fact, gave us the responsibility of assuring that they were guided into the most efficient part of our system. Therefore, that policy choice is a very important one in our process.

The last thing we had to decide was how we would pay for it. That is a struggle we all have. May I suggest that you can break all of this health care debate down into maybe one statement—that is, that you really have two choices. You can either do better with what you have or you have to take from those who have it and give it to those who do not.

In our financing scheme, like every other financing scheme, boils down to that. We are doing a lot of insurance reform. I just announced raising premiums so that more people will have it. There obviously will be more tax dollars go into this as we go along and there will obviously be some cost shifting.

Our whole plan is based from saying, let us get more in the top category, which is doing more with what we have and fewer into cost shifting. I will not go into more details. But we think our financing proposition is really straightforward and rather honest.

The plan includes the creation of some State formed buying coops, a very aggressive dose of insurance reform. We are solving the problem on pre-existing condition and guaranteed renewability and we are taking on guaranteed issue and community rating and trying to narrow the differences in premiums. All of those are in place and moving forward.

Now, let me get down to what I said I wanted to talk about today and that is tools. The biggest single variable in all of our Health Print dilemma is the fact that we need tools to get this done. Let me give you an example.

We are going to pass a pre-existing condition law this year in our State and a guaranteed renewability. But, you know, it only applies to about 30 percent of the people in my State because the rest of them are under ERISA plans and I cannot solve that problem without some help from you.

We also were very, very aggressive in terms of our cost containment activities. We have hospitals in our State, and I suspect there are others around the country, where if you go into an emergency room the physician attending you can take your basic symptoms and a number of pieces of information like your gender and your age and come up on a database, produce a whole group of options they would have in treatment. Not just what the options were, but how many people in that hospital and in that health system had been treated in that way, but what the least favorable cost was and the most favorable outcome.

Now that is at the heart of this whole debate. But very few people in our State have access to that information. So as a State we are building a wide area network that will connect all of not just our schools and our government installations but also our health care facilities that would put at the fingertip of every physician in our State that kind of cost quality data.

Now you have to finance that in some way. A lot of discussions as to how we finance it. One of the ways that is proposed is for us to deploy a quarter of 1 percent premium tax, and to put that into our quality management. We believe it would save literally millions of dollars.

But, you know, we cannot do that now. We cannot do it because we do not have any capacity to reach 70 percent of those who are in our State health system because they are under ERISA plans. We need waivers. We need some flexibility.

I will join the chorus of those saying, we need some flexibility in our Medicaid. Frankly, that is a hodge podge system. Now I have to confess to you I am new to this. I have only been in the public sector a year.

Shortly after I became Governor from the business community I went to sit down with a caseworker in my State. She had a group of files about this big and she just reached into the middle and pulled one out and she said, I remember this one.

This is a 33-year-old woman with three children. She came to me a little over a year ago and she did not have a job. We gave her AFDC and it was $419.02. We gave her food stamps for $198 and we gave her Medicaid.

Well, a short time later we put her through a training program and she got a job, paying about $6 an hour. She did not have any health benefits, so Medicaid allowed us to extend Medicaid for a year.

Well, she is back in the stack because it is now 11 months and 15 days later. She discovered that she cannot provide health care for her children and so she has done virtually the only thing she thought she could do—she has quit her job.

Well, I said, a smart guy from the private sector—we ought to be able to solve that problem. Why do we not take part of the $419 we are not having to pay her now and just pay for Medicaid to go on or some portion of it until we can phase her out. She said that would be a great idea, but, Governor, we cannot do that.

We cannot do it because of Federal regulations defining how this program works. Now that is a story you have heard repeated many different times in many different ways and you have experienced it yourself. But those are the barriers that we are seeing as a State in being able to solve our portion of this health care crisis.

Now may I suggest that we as a State cannot solve this problem on our own. We think we can get a long ways. We have the good fortune of having all but 11 percent of our citizens covered by some form of health care today. I think as Governor and as a State we can get that up to the 96 or 97 percent rate with this program, given the flexibility and the tools. But we will need some participation from the Federal Government and what we will refer to as a flexible framework and some financing mechanisms that only you can do.

Now let me close by just telling you one other thing that I feel strongly has been placed into this document. One day I was driving in from our ranch in a little county in the central part of the State called Wayne County, down in my home in Cedar City. I took what we call in our parts the Cacherom Shortcut, which is from——

The CHAIRMAN. Now we are going to have to get that term defined, too. [Laughter.]

Governor LEAVITT. The Cacherom Shortcut is a dirt road that leads from the ranch down to Cacherom, but it leads across a long, flat part of some alfalfa fields.

When I got down there the wind had blown the snow across the road. I looked at it and I was driving an old 1964 Buick Riviera with front-wheel drive. I thought to myself, I can get through just about anything with this car. So I foolishly backed up about 150 yards and took a run at that snow bank and drove into it about 150 yards and came to an absolute grinding halt.

I got out of my car and sunk up to my knees in snow and walked up over a little ridge and looked at the fact that that snow drift carried on for probably another quarter of a mile and it got nothing but deeper. Well, I was stuck and I was moving back and forth trying to—and fortunately one of our Utah Department of Transportation Trucks saw my dilemma and came down and pulled me out.

But I tell you that story because I believe that in this whole health care arena we have the prospect of driving into some snow drifts. We do not know how deep they are or how far they go. There are a lot of untried solutions being talked about out there as though they are the absolute solution. And the truth is, nobody knows how deep those snowdrifts are, how far they go.

What is going on right now in States is a very clear and I think reasonable process where we are trying to find our way through snowdrifts and there is a lot that can be learned from what is going on. But we need to have some tools. We need to have some time tables and we need to have some flexible framework.

I submit to you that the policy statement put forward by the National Governors' Association provides some first steps that you can take this year that would help us immensely.

Thank you.

The CHAIRMAN. We thank you, Governor Leavitt, very much. We would like, if I may, to put the Utah Health Print in the record of this hearing so it would be available to others.

[The document appears in the appendix.]

[The prepared statement of Governor Leavitt appears in the appendix.]

The CHAIRMAN. I welcome Senator Bennett to the Finance Committee. It is very nice to have you here, sir.

Senator BENNETT. I simply came to listen to our Governor in whom I always stand in awe. Thank you.

The CHAIRMAN. I would put in a friendly word for the Utah Department of Transportation also. [Laughter.]

Now our two distinguished leaders have come to us. Last Tuesday we all had opening statements and we said that that would be it for each of us. But neither Senator Mitchell nor Senator Dole was able to be present then. They are present now.

Senator Mitchell, would you like to make a general statement at this point; and then Senator Dole.

Senator MITCHELL. Mr. Chairman, I thank you very much. I do have a statement for the meeting. But I would prefer to place it in the record and perhaps expedite matters, utilize the time for questioning if that is agreeable.

The CHAIRMAN. That is entirely agreeable.

[The prepared statement of Senator Mitchell appears in the appendix.]

The CHAIRMAN. Senator Dole, you said the same earlier I think.

Senator DOLE. I have a very good statement, which would probably be better in the record than stated. [Laughter.]

The CHAIRMAN. Here we go. Senator Packwood, questions?

Senator PACKWOOD. I want to get clear this difference between access and coverage. Let me use Social Security as an example. The current rate is 6.2 percent on employers and employees. The law, the Federal law, says Mr., Ms. Employer, you must provide it; and to the employee, you must have it. You have no option. That is a mandate and it gets universal coverage.

If we were to say to the employer, you must make it available at 6.2 percent for you and the employee and the employee has an option to take it or not that would be access as I understand it. The employer must offer it, but the employee does not necessarily have to take it.

Before I proceed further, would that be a fair difference in your minds between universal coverage and universal access?

Governor CAMPBELL. Speaking strictly from insurance, yes, sir, that would be a fair explanation. Speaking from the standpoint of whether the health care itself was available, I do not think it would.

Senator PACKWOOD. I agree. You are right, the fact that it is 75 miles away and no doctor, it does not make much difference whether you have coverage or not.

Governor DEAN. I think I would add to that that if an individual cannot afford their portion of the 6.2 percent that really is not universal access. So I prefer not to split hairs between what access is and what coverage is.

In fact, in one of the bills the committee is considering there is an individual mandate now. When we were working this out, we found that we were getting hung up on these words and in the end they really were so similar that we decided not to argue much about what they meant.

I know what Carroll does not like. He does not like an employer mandate. He knows what I think we have to have, that is somehow everybody has to be in this system and I think that we do not want to spend too much time arguing about what access was and coverage was at least between us when we were trying to hammer this thing out.

Governor CHILES. I do not know what you want to call it, but unless everybody has it——[Laughter.]

I cannot close the gap in my State.

Governor LEAVITT. Senator, we have other access dilemmas in State Government. We struggle to give access to higher education, for example, to all of our citizens. Students argue with me often that the way we deal with that sometimes is we let them into the University but they cannot get any classes because they are all full. They refer to the macro access and micro access, all part of the same things.

I think Governor Chiles has made a very good point—we ought to be talking about what our results are and not what our process is.

Senator PACKWOOD. Well, forgetting for the moment whether we have some other limitations like unavailability of the doctors or unavailability of classes, we had six witnesses on Tuesday all of whom agreed with the statement that we will not get universal coverage without compelling it. Call it a mandate.

Now you could compel it on individuals like you do auto insurance. You could compel it on employers like we do Social Security or Worker's Comp. But you will not get what Lawton is trying to achieve without compulsion. I use the word instead of mandate. It is a stronger word.

The CHAIRMAN. Can you not say statute? [Laughter.]

Senator PACKWOOD. I am curious if you would agree with that conclusion. It does not necessarily mean we are going to do it, but that we will not get what Lawton hopes to achieve unless we say it must be done.

Governor CHILES. I agree.

Senator PACKWOOD. Governor Dean?

Governor DEAN. I think I agree with that, yes.

Senator PACKWOOD. Governor Campbell?

Governor CAMPBELL. I would agree with one caveat. Hawaii has universal coverage and they do not cover all their people.

Senator PACKWOOD. They have 94 percent, but you are right.

Governor CAMPBELL. Ninety-four percent. They do not cover all their people. If you look at the chronically uninsured and deal with that group in a different way, you have a lot of other steps you can use to get there.

Governor LEAVITT. And I would agree with Governor Campbell. There is very good evidence that you could have an employer mandate and still not have universal coverage.

Senator PACKWOOD. You may come closer than anything else. Actually, you would come closer with an individual mandate if you said the individual had to have it and if you were below a certain line we will help finance it with credits.

Governor LEAVITT. And it may be that at some point in time we will discover that is an absolute necessity. But we are a long ways from that point yet. We could probably learn a great deal from universal access about what would be produced by universal coverage.

Senator PACKWOOD. That was the argument we learned in Minnesota the other day, the extraordinary success they have had with the universal access but not a mandate.

Governor DEAN. Senator, I should make one point. In our bill in Vermont, which we are hopefully going to enact at the end of this year, we, in fact, did recognize that and we would have both an employer mandate and for those who are self-employed and unemployed an individual mandate. We will help them pay for it. But we do expect some responsibility on their part as well.

But ours really runs more like Social Security than it does, say, automobile insurance.

Senator PACKWOOD. Let me go now to the State variances, because I think Governor Dean you said in terms of national tort reform, I think you used the words broad national outline with State variance. Do I quote you roughly?

Governor DEAN. That is the NGA position.

Senator PACKWOOD. All right.

Governor DEAN. If you were tough enough, I would be perfectly happy to have the feds do the whole thing.

Senator PACKWOOD. I was going to ask you in terms of the NGA position what that exactly means—national tort reform with a sort of a broad national outline, but then State variances.

Governor DEAN. I do not have our position right in front of us. But to my recollection we wanted to talk about things the Federal Government might be willing to do. We are kind of hung up in the same problem the Federal Government is on this one. I think we are looking at the Federal Government as the Utah Department of Transportation in this one. [Laughter.]

You know, the question is, are we going to have a battle with the trial lawyers in one place or are we going to have it in 50 different places. Now the reason that we are a little fuzzy in this position, frankly, is that this has been traditionally a domain of the States and obviously Governors are reluctant to give up any of their domain.

On the other hand, we also, from a practical point of view, think it is probably more practical to have one fight in Washington than it is to have 50 fights in all the State Capitals. So in candor, unless Carroll as the Chairman would like to be a little bit more specific, I would say that our position is a little fuzzy because we do not quite agree.

There are many of us, probably Carroll and I both agree on this thing, that would be very pleased for a very tough national framework which might even include such things as caps on pain and suffering and so forth. But at a minimum I would think it would include mandatory arbitration and things of that sort.

Governor CAMPBELL. That is basically what our policy is calling for, an alternative dispute resolution.

Senator PACKWOOD. Thank you, Mr. Chairman.

The CHAIRMAN. Thank you, Senator Packwood.

Thank you, Governors Campbell and Dean. I think we have a clear proposition before us.

Senator Mitchell?

Senator MITCHELL. Mr. Chairman, thank you very much.

Thank you, Senator Baucus. My other colleague is permitting me to go at this time in the questioning.

I would like to continue the line of inquiry begun by Senator Packwood because I think it is the central issue. The figure of 94 percent was—the Governor has said 98 percent; others have said 96 percent. While there may be some disagreement on the numbers, may we not all agree that between 94 and 98 percent is better than 75 percent?

Governor CAMPBELL. True.

Senator MITCHELL. And do the other Governors share the view expressed by Governor Chiles and by many witnesses before this committee? Governor Chiles' words were, "You cannot control costs unless you have universal coverage." I believe he was expressing the view that the two are intimately related and effective achievement of one objective requires the other.

So I will ask each of the other Governors—Governor Dean, Governor Campbell, Governor Leavitt—do you agree with that ascertain by Governor Chiles?

Governor DEAN. I absolutely agree with it. It is a very difficult, thorny question. There is no question about it, that if you do not include everybody you cannot control costs. And it goes to the question of the global budget.

I understand all the objections on an ideological basis to price controls and all those kinds of things, many of which I agree with. But the problem is, that unless you control costs by having everybody in the system and then controlling costs; and then unless you control costs in the whole system, there is a terrible cost shift. So first of all, everybody has to be in the system to get rid of some of that cost shift.

Secondly, I am very willing to listen to alternatives to global budgets. I have told the business community in our State, if you do not want a global budget, I will not put one on you because I know the business community hates global budgets. But the fact of the matter is, in the people that we cover, we are not going to allow our costs to go up at 11 percent or 9 percent a year. We are going to cap that.

And if we cap that and you do not have a global budget your expenses are going to go up because the medical industry is going to shift those costs to you. So it is a very difficult one, because ideologically our business people are like business people everywhere. They do not believe in government price controls and so forth and they have seen that they have not worked in the past.

But they also know that Medicaid and Medicare are rapidly shifting the cost to them like crazy. I am going to be very interested to see what they have to say when this bill gets in the end stage in the Conference Committee. If you do not have everybody in, you cannot control costs.

So far I have not been able to think of a way that you can control costs to the public sector if you do not control costs for the private sector.

Senator MITCHELL. Governor Campbell?

Governor CAMPBELL. I think you have universal coverage now in the worst possible way, that is that people can go into the hospital and get help for nothing because hospitals must serve them and they shift the cost over to someone else.

So I think that you need universal coverage for delivery of health care to people. Inclusive in that definition has got to be the public health component that we are going to have to utilize to deliver this. It is not there unless we include the public health component.

Now you might be able to design a system which replaces for instance our costs of running a health department or other things that we are now doing to provide service by having a fee payment back through a system, whatever system you have, for insurance to those public health entities that would allow a cost shift out and net out a basis that is not going to run up costs.

But I do think that you have to recognize that no matter what you do, we are going to have to have a public health component. And that no matter how good we are, whether it is 96, 98, or 94 percent, there is going to be a subset of people out there that are going to fall through the cracks and there is going to have to be a public health component. So within that context I would agree with you.

Senator MITCHELL. Governor Leavitt?

Governor LEAVITT. Senator, yesterday I had the good pleasure of testifying before a similar committee with Governor Waihee from Hawaii, who we spoke of today in terms of his system.

It was interesting to me as we sat at the table I had placed in front of me a table on the percentage of average family income that is spent on health care, keeping in mind that we have radically different systems and, frankly, radically different opinions as to how it should be approached.

Well, I looked down the list and I find that number 43 is Utah, spending 10.2 percent of our family income and number 44 is Hawaii, spending 10 percent. So out of every $100 that a person in my State and their State spends there is 20 cents difference in the amount that we spend on health care.

I think Governor Campbell is correct that we have in the worst possible way today a sense of universal coverage. The question is, is it being provided in the best type of quality and is the financing mechanism correct.

So I am not sure that cost containment is directly linked to employee mandate. I think there are many other factors involved and I think these would demonstrate that.

Senator MITCHELL. Thank you.

On a separate issue, Governor Campbell, in your prepared statement I believe you said, and I want to verify this, that you are opposed to a cap on Medicaid spending without restructuring the system. Is that correct?

Governor CAMPBELL. Yes, sir.

Senator MITCHELL. So if in his budget President Clinton proposes a cap on Medicaid spending without restructuring the system you would urge us to oppose that effort?

Governor CAMPBELL. I would, because if we have a cap, and I will just be very blunt, what our policy is that we see a cost shift that is going to come down that we would have to deal with without the ability to restructure the system and without ability to have the flexibility to do the things we want to go into managed care and things of that nature. We cannot effect the savings.

Senator MITCHELL. And so, therefore, logically if anyone else proposed a cap on Medicaid without restructuring the system, say a member of this committee or someone in the Senate, you would urge us to oppose that as well.

Governor CAMPBELL. I would look at all of these different plans in here and where there is a cap, if we do not have the flexibility to restructure a system we do not think we can affect savings and there will be changes that will push costs down.

Senator MITCHELL. Right. I thank you. I see my time is up. I have other questions. I am going to stay and try to get into another round. Mr. Chairman, thank you.

The CHAIRMAN. Sure.

Senator Dole?

Senator DOLE. I think the question has already been answered. But I assume in all your States everybody can receive treatment, is that correct? Nobody can be turned away if they have a medical problem.

The CHAIRMAN. Could I make the statement that the record does not records nods. [Laughter.]

Governor CAMPBELL. Yes, Senator.

The CHAIRMAN. Let us go across.

Governor CAMPBELL. Yes.

Governor DEAN. Yes.

Governor CHILES. Yes.

Governor LEAVITT. Yes.

Senator DOLE. Well, I think it is a point that some people fail to understand. I think you talked about coverage or access or whatever, but it is not the best way to do it, as the Governor of Utah has pointed out. It is probably the most expensive way.

But it does make the point that at least in America we have a pretty good system. We do not want to destroy that system in the process of trying to cure it. There are a lot of good people out there that have different views. I think in a few months we will be voting on what will be the consensus of hopefully this committee and 75 or 80 members of the Senate, maybe more.

Did it take very long for the Democrat and Republican Governors to reach your sort of consensus? Did you have any debate?

Governor CAMPBELL. Yes, sir, we had a lot of debate. As a matter of fact, we started this debate and Governor Dean and I were just looking at some of the items that we had up in 1992, very similar to what we have now. We have gone through a rather lengthy process of debating all of the issues back and forth.

Quite frankly, we have moved a little bit along the way. It has been a rather slow process, but we have moved or at least evolved to the point of where we are today.

Senator DOLE. Would it be fair to characterize the Governors' action as sort of incremental reform? How would you characterize your package?

Governor CAMPBELL. Well, our package recognizes specific items as a whole that need to be done. Incremental in that would be getting Medicaid under managed care and doing the things that can affect savings and things of that nature.

But in our general package we call for the alliances. I have a bill pending in my legislature right now to allow alliances of small business groups that want to provide a mechanism to purchase insurance. It is a voluntary mechanism that we want to put in. We do not call for mandatory alliances.

We are specific on employer mandates. We are specific in the three areas that we disagree on. Employer mandates, and the global budgeting, and the price controls.

Governor LEAVITT. Senator, could I comment on that, Senator Dole?

Senator DOLE. Sure.

Governor LEAVITT. Virtually every plan that I have seen coming out of a State depends in some way on the capacity to restructure and create savings. That would be true, I think, of most of the Federal plans if not all.

The difference that I believe should be focused on between State plans and the Federal plan is that almost every State plan depends on those savings actually having been realized before they are spent. And there is serious concern, at least on the part of this Governor and I believe on many others, that those savings the Federal Government will project will not ultimately materialize, but that the Federal Government will not have to worry about it because they will have assurity. They will have a guarantor.

And that guarantor will be States. That is the major concern that at least I have and why we urge an incremental approach, a blueprint approach, as opposed to putting us all into what I have heard referred to as the big bang theory, where it all has to happen at one moment and then we will fix it after that. That is a real concern at least for this Governor and I believe others.

Governor DEAN. Well, Senator, if I may read the first line of our official policy—"The nation's Governors are committed to a comprehensive health reform."

Now there are a lot of different definitions of comprehensive health reform. I certainly believe the Chafee bill, for example, is a comprehensive health reform. So we may not agree on exactly——

Senator CHAFEE. Wait a minute. Did you say you thought it was or it was not?

Governor DEAN. Was.

Senator CHAFEE. Thank you. [Laughter.]

Governor DEAN. There are certainly different forms of comprehensive health reform. But I do not think we plan to do this piece by piece. We do hope that whatever comes out is a comprehensive piece.

Senator DOLE. If we did all the things the Governors suggest that would be comprehensive health care.

Governor DEAN. Well, it would be comprehensive, although there are some things that we left out. The piece we have not yet agreed on is the financing piece and that needs to be done. We have not agreed on it and maybe we will.

Governor CHILES. I really think we are characterizing it wrong. I believe to call this the—this is not the Governors' health plan. This is the Governors' wish list to say these are the things that we hope that at least you will allow us to do.

It is not a complete plan. Each one of the Governors has a Governor's health plan. I can certainly give you mine. But this statement which I voted on and voted for, I certainly did not vote for that and say here is our health plan to go with the Chafee plan, the Breaux plan, the President's plan. This is a list of things that we think should be allowed in a comprehensive plan.

Senator DOLE. In any plan.

Governor CHILES. So incremental is not, I do not think, a fair approach to it. Now every time we meet we come up with something else we would like to put on the list because it is something that we are trying in our States. But I do not think it is a Governors' health plan.

Senator DOLE. In any plan.

Governor CAMPBELL. Senator, could I mention one thing? I want to remind you that Senator Chiles is right, in that we did not sit down and say this is the plan you should pass. This is components of it. But we call for insurance reform and we call for purchasing cooperatives. That is part of virtually every other plan. We call for core benefits and access and that is part of most everybody's plan. We call for tax deductibility on health care premiums. That is in dispute among some people, but the Governors call for it equally.

We call for low income subsidies as a way to bridge the gap of those working poor and we call for changes to the current Medicaid system. And we do call for medical malpractice and liability reform and antitrust statutes, relief from ERISA, federally organized outcome and quality standards. We do not have a database to go from to do some of these things. And administrative simplifications.

81-991 O - 94 - 3

Now to some degree or another these components are, if you take some of the plans, you can pull some of these out of at least one or more of those plans. So, therefore, it does go down to a lot of what an overall plan would finally accomplish.

Senator DOLE. Could I just ask one additional question?

The CHAIRMAN. Please.

Senator DOLE. I mentioned in my statement we had a very good discussion with Republican Governors and leadership in the House and the Senate. Without getting into names of different plans there was one particular plan that concerned I think you, Governor Campbell, because the additional cost to South Carolina for the Medicaid program.

Governor CAMPBELL. Yes, sir. The problem that we are looking at is one of the plans proposes that the feds take acute care and we take long term care. We think that ought to be reversed. We have looked at it very carefully as we looked at the whole plan to determine, you know, how it would impact us.

I think it is important for you to recognize that in drawing these conclusions that what has happened is that we do not think that certain dynamics have been taken into consideration. That is our biggest problem here. We think that it ought to go the other way.

There are concerns with other parts of this, too, in the Clinton plan, which is another plan on Medicaid. That calls for maintenance of effort. Well, the data that we have show that the growth of Medicaid now is abating and may be as low as 8 percent this year and the savings that they are talking about may not be there. And if you lock us in a maintenance effort, and effort that is too high, it, in fact, would cause us to be spending money in a mandated way when, in fact, we may need it in other parts of a plan.

Senator DOLE. Without mentioning the Breaux plan by name, do all Governors share that view, at least with respect to Medicaid.

The CHAIRMAN. Without mentioning the Breaux plan by name. [Laughter.]

Governor DEAN. That plan is a great concern to Governors because it does appear to be a federally centralized plan with little flexibility for States, little opportunity for States to be more efficient at their own level in addition to the problems that Governor Campbell has raised. So that would be a particularly alarming development for us, for all Governors, both Republicans and Democrats, should that plan be not significantly modified.

Governor CHILES. I do not want to nod on that one because I can tell you, Florida with its percent of elderly people if you say we are going to take long term care and that is our responsibility, we lost one battle when we tried to succeed, but we would have to try again. [Laughter.]

The CHAIRMAN. Can I just point out that we have a vote that is now in its last 5 minutes. Before we close down, just the spirit in which Senator Dole is speaking, we are trying to reach the kind of consensus that you have reached. We are not going to be in complete agreement. But I think Senator Dole said it in some months hence we are going to have 75 or 80 Senators agreed on a health care measure. I think that is a nice note on which to go off and vote on something, a probable question which we have not yet dealt with.

Senator ROTH. Mr. Chairman, are we going to be able to submit questions?

The CHAIRMAN. Of course you are and we are coming back. I wonder if the Governors would not like to sit back here. There is coffee available. We will be back in about 5 minutes.

[Whereupon, at 11:51 a.m., the hearing recessed, to resume at 12:00 p.m.]

The CHAIRMAN. The committee will resume its hearing.

Senator Baucus, you are next.

Senator BAUCUS. Thank you, Mr. Chairman.

I would like to try to stay on what I regard as the main focus. Senator Packwood asked some questions along those lines as did Senator Mitchell. Essentially, it is just to reconfirm my understanding that you, Governor Chiles and Governor Dean, agree that we are going to have comprehensive coverage, and community rating, although that raises certain other questions.

Do we need some form of required participation? I understood Governor Chiles and Governor Dean to say yes, if you are going to have universal coverage you do need to have some kind of required participation in the system.

As I heard you, Governor Campbell and Governor Leavitt, you are not quite sure. Could you expand on that? The two Governors to your right seem to believe that to get a handle on this we do need some form of required participation otherwise you get the cost shifting and you can't get real cost containment.

How do you get from here to there without some form of required participation?

Governor CAMPBELL. I think there is something that we all—and I have made this point before—need to understand. Hawaii, depending on whose figures, 4, 5 or 6 percent are uninsured that are in their system. They have a full coverage system. And in Minnesota where they do not have a mandate, there are about 7 or 8 percent that are uninsured.

So when you reach that point, the question then becomes one of cost.

Senator BAUCUS. That is the next question I was going to ask.

Governor CAMPBELL. Yes. Can you go the last 4 or 5 percent in the cost with all the mandates or are you going to have to pick that up with the public health system that we have now?

That is the reason I kept saying we have to count the public health component as part of this overall coverage.

Senator BAUCUS. Governor Leavitt, how can we deal with comprehensive coverage and costs without some form of required participation?

Governor LEAVITT. One thing I believe we will agree upon is that that last 3 or 4 or 5 percent of access will require some form of Federal mechanism in order to provide for the income redistribution that will take place in that proposition.

I believe as Governor Campbell that there are many systems, the one I have proposed as well in my own State, that I believe will bring us to that 95 or 96 percent that once we get to that point in our own plan—we are saying at this point we have to decide if we need an employer mandate to go any further.

I am not convinced that there are not other systems that will provide that. I just think it is a lot better to do that and try it and see what we have as opposed to—you know, I think the employer mandate is a good example of the snow bank I talked about earlier. I am not sure we know exactly what that is going to produce.

Senator BAUCUS. Let me just tell you what one of my questions, concerns is about all this. I am sure it is one of yours. We can kind of think our way through it. That is, it is cost.

Now you talk about the public participation picking up the remainder, whatever it is. Well, that to me gets to the question of cost. I assume some sort of subsidy and Federal Government—well, State Governments would be paying.

I think one of the reasons we are all here today, and certainly why the Governors were in town addressing health care, is cost. It is cost to State Government. I know in my State, the Medicaid budget is the largest single component of the State budget and it exceeds the total cost that the State pays for the University of Montana and Montana State University combined. It is just getting so bad.

So the question I have is, assuming we all agree on universal coverage, two of you think we have to have some kind of required participation and I hear the other two saying there are other ways to get it, require some and leave, some voluntary.

But then what about costs? I do not see that we have solved the cost component yet without some sort of cost control. I was struck in the Governors' budget that you are not for enforceable budgets. I know all Governors are very proud that they have to balance budgets. You know, we hear that all the time from Governors.

I am just curious. It just seems to me that unless there is some meaningful way to address costs, we are going to have business costs. Health care costs are going to continue to go up, even though we have some universal coverage and maybe some kind of required participation, and State and Federal budgets are going to go up because we are going to have, in effect, a kind of entitlement program that is just not going to address the cost.

Governor CHILES. I just want to clarify a little bit, you know, the statement that I made or that I would be in agreement to, having to have some kind of mandates. If you want to put the tax holds in there, you know, and rather than the last 3 or 4 percent, as Mike has said in Utah, we are looking at the last 12 percent, I think 10 to 12 percent in Florida. We cannot close it more than that.

Now if you want to say you are going to give us the tax money to cover all these people, yes, we do not need a mandate. I will work on that. But do not ask to share in that.

The CHAIRMAN. I would like to cut off this line of questioning right away. [Laughter.]

Senator BAUCUS. But we are not going to provide unlimited tax dollars, so then what?

Governor CHILES. Then we do not have a match.

Governor DEAN. Senator, I think one of the things we all agree on wherever we are on the employer mandate is that there has to be some individual component to this, except for the very poorest of the poor. Everybody has to contribute something. There are three places you are going to get the money.

You are going to get the money from the employers. How much we have not agreed on. You are going to get the money from the taxpayers. And you are going to get the money from the individuals.

We all agree that the individuals have to pay something. So at some level there is going to be an individual mandate whether it is the one that Senator Chafee described in his bill or whether it is just a matter of co-payments or whatever it is.

I think all the Governors understand that individuals have to contribute something to their health care and an entitlement program is not something the Governors would want, and I suspect it is not something that the Senators would want either—an uncapped entitlement program.

Senator BAUCUS. I know my time has expired. I just have not heard any of you really address the question—the need for cost controls. I

Governor DEAN. I believe in global budgets.

Senator BAUCUS. Well, it is a Governor's statement.

Governor CAMPBELL. I will tell you why Howard can believe in a balanced budget for Vermont and I believe in it in South Carolina and have it my Constitution and I have to do it.

Senator BAUCUS. Right.

Governor CAMPBELL. But I control that budget. I do not control what Federal programs are pushed down upon my budget; I have no control whatsoever over that. And, therefore, I cannot support a global budget set at the top which can cost shift down to the States.

Senator BAUCUS. Would you if there is no cost shift?

Governor CAMPBELL. I beg your pardon?

Senator BAUCUS. Would you if there is no cost shift or to use another phrase, unfunded mandates and all that, would you then?

Governor CAMPBELL. Well, we have tried to get them. I have not seen them yet.

Senator BAUCUS. But in principle.

Governor CAMPBELL. In principle, if we have a partnership with the Federal Government in a particular program, we could deal with it. But we have that partnership in Medicaid and it has not exactly worked all that well.

I think we need to understand one of the main reasons that we have "an insurance crisis" is that the Federal programs—Medicaid, and to a lesser extent the Medicare program—have cost shifted, as those programs have been liberalized, to the private sector and that has run up the cost of private insurance.

That is the reason that you hear all of us talking about getting this Medicaid program into managed care so we can bring down this cost shift. And a lot of us are already working on it. That is the reason I said a moment ago that some of the savings that the President is counting on to finance his plan are not going to be there. We have already gotten it down to about an 8 percent growth we think this year, down from 12 to 14 percent growth.

Senator BAUCUS. Thank you.

The CHAIRMAN. And I think I heard you agree with, Governor Campbell, on the fact that the Medicaid——

Senator BAUCUS. Absolutely.

The CHAIRMAN. I think, Governors, we recognize what you are saying here.

Under our rather arcane arrangements, our next questioner is Senator Riegle.

Senator RIEGLE. Thank you very much, Mr. Chairman. I appreciate the work and the time of the Governors that are here today.

Hawaii is not represented here today, but in effect it is at the table. I found some facts about Hawaii to be quite interesting that I would like to relate to today's discussion and ask you to react to it.

When Hawaii started their, in effect, universal health care system about 20 years ago, they were in a somewhat unique position. And also out where they are, it is not as if people or businesses could move next door into a neighboring State.

When we look at the cost issue and come back to what Senator Baucus is raising, because that gets to who pays and taxes, and gets into the very hard question of how we pay for whatever it is we want to do here, I am struck by the Hawaii experience. When they went to universal coverage it took about 10 years before the cost lines began to break apart between the cost efficiency of that universal system versus the rest of the United States.

Then from year 10 to year 20 it widened out. The last data that I saw showed that Hawaii was spending about 8 percent of its economy on health care while the rest of the country, the United States, was spending about 14 percent. So that it took 10 years for the cost lines to break apart, but then they really did break apart and now the State has nearly universal coverage, but at a much lower cost.

I asked why that was so and was told that it is partly gearing in the system. But costs are lower also because they are now getting better health outcomes, that a good system of universal coverage with good preventive care over time gives you fewer sick people. You find things earlier, you prevent certain things, and as a result, the health profile of people in Hawaii now looks better.

I asked a question about 50-year-old white males, as an example. If you look category by category do you really see better outcomes in comparable groups? Because we think of Hawaii as a place with just a little less stress, that is a little more serene, and maybe people just get healthier out there.

But they were arguing that if you took comparable demographic groups that they actually have been able to measure a health improvement over time by the virtue of the fact that everybody is covered. The problem that we are boxed into here is we have these 5-year budgets.

Whatever we decide to do and however we pay for it, we have to finance it and plug it into the Federal budget system over the 5-year period of time, as Senator Chiles remembers all too well.

But the real cost efficiencies are going to show up later, and some of them are going to show up in the private sector, which we do not even try to work into our calculations of public expenditures.

Businesses, for example, are going to save some money if they are now eating all of the cost shifted premiums.

So the question is, how do we come up with the money to pay for something where the real benefits may show up beyond this 5-year time window.

I ask you to help us think about that because when we finally resolve the issue of what we can do and what we cannot do, we are going to have to pay for it. And Senator Moynihan, Chairman Moynihan, has raised this question before—you know, where does the money come from, how much is it.

We may have to ask your help to look at costs and benefits over a longer time frame, costs and benefits, than just this arbitrary 5-year window. We may end up doing the wrong things because we are in a budget straightjacket that really does not look at how the economics play out over time.

Governor Campbell, could you react to that?

Governor CAMPBELL. I think your point is well taken. It is difficult to spend money before you get it, even though it has been done quite often.

The CHAIRMAN. We found a way to do it.

Governor CAMPBELL. I understand. But under the other new constraints it is going to be a difficult situation. It is going to take time to affect a lot of the savings. There is no question about that.

Hawaii has a number of unique features. Not only did they go to employer mandates, they are not under ERISA. I want to point that out. Governor Dean has mentioned a time or two that we have problems there because we cannot even deal with minimum policies offered in ERISA and they may be less than the policies we offer. So that is something that everybody needs to look at.

The prevention side of it will save money. There is no question about it. That is the reason many of us have launched the massive immunization programs, pregnancy prevention programs—I—we are in a children having children situation which is feeding our public health system and creating other huge problems.

And as we look at these things, we have to understand, if we get the Medicaid people into front end medicine and primary care, where they get into prevention, we are going to over time affect savings. We are not going to affect them the first year or the second year. You will see savings slowly come in as you change the pattern of care.

The preventive side of it, primary care, moving out of the hospital emergency rooms, and getting better health care is going to take time to show results. There is no question.

Senator RIEGLE. Governor Dean?

Governor DEAN. Senator, I may have some good news for you. I think, frankly, that Hawaii's health outcomes may have had some influence. But one of the reasons Hawaii has had the outcomes it has is because essentially they have an alliance system already in place. They have two insurers of significance in the private sector and only two.

And under the Clinton proposal with the big alliances controlling the market, I think you are going to see cost reduction or a reduction in the rate of increase much faster than you did in Hawaii, which had a significant amount of market consolidation as a result of their employer mandate in 1974.

So I think you can expect savings because of the concentration of buying power which I believe, even though the folks from Hawaii do not talk about that very much, has a significant impact.

In Vermont our costs are 48th in the country. We have two insurers of significance. One is an HMO; one is Blue Cross/Blue Shield. The same kind of situation in Hawaii where they have combined services, which is Blue Cross/Blue Shield and Kaiser handling almost the entire private market. Then, of course, the government programs which are cost capped anyway.

So I think you can under the President's plan expect to see savings much more quickly. I think to a certain extent that has been actually tried in Hawaii because those two insurance companies function as alliances, somewhat similarly to alliances under the President's plan.

Senator RIEGLE. Could I ask just one follow-up?

The CHAIRMAN. Please do.

Senator RIEGLE. I will be very brief. Let us say that is right. Let us say we have some experience now that suggests that we can start to earn savings from the front end investment of going to a more universal system. The question is, will we get there within a 5-year time frame?

Governor DEAN. Probably not.

Senator RIEGLE. You see, that is the point.

Governor DEAN. But I think it will not be 10 years. I think you will see some of it in 5 years.

Senator RIEGLE. But here is the problem. We are locked into a set of budget rules here that are very diabolical in the sense that they force us to make the numbers balance within that time frame. And, in fact, I think what we may need here perhaps is a 10-year time frame.

Now some people say that is just a dodge. That it is an effort to escape the discipline. But what I hear you all saying is that to do this right and to measure it right, 5 years just is too short a time frame, especially if you are going to front load the system by bringing in people who are not now covered, and start them in a managed care relationship that provides preventive care.

So we may have to, in fact, invent for this one issue a way in which we measure this over a 10-year time frame. That leads then to the financing decisions being different. And if we try to do it in this arbitrary 5-year time frame, we may be headed for a train wreck here.

Governor LEAVITT. Senator, could I make a comment on this?

Senator RIEGLE. Please, Senator Leavitt.

Governor LEAVITT. It is of concern to me that we might attribute all of Hawaii's success to an employer mandate. I mean, Hawaii's percentage of their total personal income is at 10 percent. I have a figure right here. My own State is at 10.2 percent and there are six States that are better than Hawaii with respect to the amount of the percentage of their income, and all of those States have had made progress.

There are a lot of other factors that I think that could go into that. So as we think about long term——

Senator RIEGLE. There is no State that has got as high a rate of coverage as Hawaii. There is nobody that is close.

Senator DURENBERGER. Minnesota is.

Senator RIEGLE. Minnesota.

Governor LEAVITT. But the same number of dollars are going into the system. I think Governor Campbell earlier mentioned the fact that there is a——

Senator RIEGLE. He is governing more people percentage wise.

The CHAIRMAN. We are going to move on. But can we just say that we talked about this in our last hearing that States are not all alike. There are different patterns and we see them in all kinds of activities—education and health.

Senator Breaux?

The CHAIRMAN. I am sorry, Governor Chiles.

Governor CHILES. I just wanted to say to my good friend Senator Riegle that you would not get too much sympathy from this group about your 5-year problem, in that we have a 1-year problem.

Senator RIEGLE. I understand.

Governor CHILES. We have a train wreck every year. And generally speaking, that is a train that, you know, the engine is coming from here that is driving our train. It wrecks every year.

Senator RIEGLE. But to the question of how this committee will fiance the front end investment for the whole country at once, we do not have an answer right now.

The CHAIRMAN. Fair enough. Well, there is a Senator. There are two here who have answers. One of them is Senator Breaux.

Senator BREAUX. Of Cooper, Cooper, Cooper, Cooper, Breaux. [Laughter.]

Senator BREAUX. Thank you very much, Mr. Chairman. You know, there is an old saying that is often repeated in Washington that if you like the final product you could not watch either laws nor sausage being made. We are right in the middle of that process. We are delighted that the Governors have decided to jump into it with us because we cannot do it without you, and nor should we try and do it without the input of the States.

I want to commend all of their testimonies and to say something to Howard Dean. Mr. Chairman, Governor Dean was our lead off witness in our first day of welfare reform hearings and did a super job telling us about what his State of Vermont is doing in the area of welfare reform. We look forward to bringing the NGA up to give their position on that issue as well as on this issue.

Let me ask just a couple of questions. Assume there was a bill that provided coverage to the people in your State who are poor, who cannot now afford insurance because they cannot afford it through subsidies; and a bill that would at the same time provide coverage for sick people, who have a pre-existing condition or have a catastrophic illness and have their insurance cancelled and also provides portability.

Assume that such protections are in effect for poor people and sick people who do not now have insurance. Who else in your State would not be covered?

Governor DEAN. In our State anybody who chose not to be covered would not be covered and that is a significant problem because it gets to the issue of what happens to a twenty-five year old young male who chooses to spend their money doing something else.

If they get in a motorcycle wreck and they do not have insurance, the taxpayers or somebody else, or the hospitals or the private sector picks up the $100,000 cost.

So just covering working people who cannot afford insurance is not enough.

Senator BREAUX. And nonworking people plus that.

Governor DEAN. And nonworking people and so forth is not enough. We have to find a way to get everybody in the system one way or the other.

Senator BREAUX. And the timing as to when they come in is also a factor. Governor Campbell, do you have a thought on that?

Governor CAMPBELL. There is no question that timing is a factor in it. Governor Dean is right. I mean, a lot of people choose not to be covered. Some of them choose for economic reasons; some of them choose for personal reasons. Some of them carry catastrophic coverage and do not carry primary coverage and things of that nature.

So there is a whole mix of people out there in this country that have made that particular choice. The ones that we have to pick up are those, I guess, that made the choice and have no means of paying for a problem. Some of them have made the choice and do have a means. We have no way of differentiating particularly.

Senator BREAUX. Some have argued in this committee and in other forums that in order to get a handle on controls of cost of health insurance we need two things. We need, number one, universal coverage; and secondly, we need a system of price controls or premium caps to keep controls on the price.

Now it seems to me that in Medicare, which the Federal Government's largest health program, that we have universal coverage. And secondly, we also have price controls. And yet last year with those two ingredients, Medicare increased over $20 billion.

Governor CAMPBELL. Your population increased.

Senator BREAUX. So my question is, if we have universal coverage in a health program and we have price controls in a health program, and we still see over a $20 billion increase in 1 year, do you have any idea about what is missing?

Senator CHAFEE. John, could you put that into percentage increase? In other words, $20 billion on what basis. I think it comes out to something like 12 or 13 percent, if I am correct.

Senator BREAUX. Probably around 12 percent.

Governor DEAN. Well, I am a very staunch advocate of totally redoing the Medicare system. I can tell you as a practicing physician and as a Governor, there is no greater scourge on States than the Health Care Financing Administration, Medicare in particular.

Senator BREAUX. Other than that, it works pretty good.

Governor DEAN. I mean what we need is capitated care, Senator. You cannot——

The CHAIRMAN. Governor, you are going to help us with our glossary—capitated care.

Governor DEAN. You have got to pay physicians based on how many patients they take care of, not what they do for those patients, because the reason your Medicare costs are out of control is every time you clamp a bureaucratic cost control on a particular service we just do more of them so we get paid the same amount.

It does not work. The Medicare system will never work to control costs unless you switch and get away from a fee-for-service system.

The CHAIRMAN. Capitated care, sir, is you take a patient and——

Governor DEAN. For example, when I was a practicing physician, which was until the day I became Governor, I was in private practice with two other physicians and we had contracts to provide an HMO and also contracts with Blue Cross and so forth. Blue Cross paid us.

If somebody came in, we did a cardiogram, urinalysis exam and so forth, we billed them for each one of those. On the other hand, the HMO paid me $10.78 per patient per month, whether I saw them 50 times and did 5 cardiograms or whether I did not see them for the whole year. There you can budget.

Now under those contexts a global budget is not intrusive at all, at least for a physician, because I know what I am going to get paid. I do not have to send any bills out at the end of the month. I do not have to have a team of bureaucrats coming in and telling me whether I kept somebody in the hospital two extra days or did not do enough cardiograms or did too many. I just get that payment.

You do have to have some people coming in to make sure I deliver decent, proper care. That you do have to have. But it is much less bureaucratic. I think a global budget in terms of Medicare would scare the daylights out of me and I would never support it.

But a global budget in terms of paying physicians by the patients, not by the service, is much less bureaucratic than what we have now at the Federal level.

Senator BREAUX. Can I have one other question?

The CHAIRMAN. Please. I interrupted you.

Senator BREAUX. I appreciate your answers. On the question of Medicaid and what we do with it, which is an immense problem, it is my understanding that under the administration's proposal on Medicaid that what we basically do is say that the States will continue to pay the share of Medicare for nonworking poor people in your State. And, therefore, the working poor that the States will somehow have to contribute to an alliance to help pay for their coverage.

Under the Cooper-Breaux plan what we have spelled out in the beginning is that the Federal Government would pick up the cost of acute care and give to the States the cost of long term health care.

Now CBO says that in the short term, that is a big savings for the State; but in the long term, 5 to 10 years, as the babyboomers become senior citizens that that can tend to reverse and that the costs become more for long term than it does for acute care.

Can you tell me what is, Carroll, the recommendation of the NGA on how that should be handled?

Governor CAMPBELL. Well, we, first on the long term care, agree with you on CBO. We think it is flawed because it assumes that only a subset of services that have traditionally been considered in long term care would be given to the States.

We are concerned about picking long-term care. We think it should be reversed if we go in that direction.

Senator BREAUX. You all would prefer that the Federal Government do long term health care the States stay with acute care?

Governor CAMPBELL. We would. I would. I assume that the others would.

The CHAIRMAN. Once again, we have that nodding.

Senator BREAUX. Yes, universal nods.

Governor CAMPBELL. Yes, we are all for that, Mr. Chairman.

There are some other questions that you asked that are very interesting about your plan and shifting and what goes to the States. That has been our concern as States with the Cooper-Breaux plan. We think it has some very good features in it.

I personally think it has some good features in it. I personally think Senator Chafee's plan has some very good features in it.

Our concern is, what happens to States under those plans, like this particular trade that was offered on acute care and long term care would not be to our benefit. There are some other items that we might happen to like in it.

So I want you to take our answers as speaking to the individual issues, as the Chairman has said, and not to the individual bills strictly dealing with the issues one at a time. And out of that, maybe we can find some long term answers.

Senator BREAUX. Most of us all realizing that the only thing we are going to be able to do is to come up with a good, solid compromise and take the best features of all the bills. I think that is what we are going to do.

Thank you, Mr. Chairman.

The CHAIRMAN. Senator Durenberger, would you like to extend the honor of the State of Minnesota with respect to coverage?

Senator DURENBERGER. Thank you. Mr. Chairman, I just want to say what I said at the last hearing. I am down to now 333 days left in this august body, from which I will thence be freed. I want to say to my poor colleagues that I will not cherish anything as much as I will my relationships with the Governors over the years. That goes back to Dick Snelling and the new federalism efforts we made and my colleague, Lawton, seeing him in that position. This has been a wonderful experience for me and I think it has been for everybody here.

I think one of the unfortunate traps we have been falling into all of the time is getting into this debate over universal coverage. One of the good things that has happened here today is we are trying to define it. I think that is very helpful.

Governor Dean, when you said unless everyone is in you cannot control costs, that is kind of the issue I need to explore with you because we began to control costs in hospitals in 1983 when we went to DRG's. We prospectively priced it. I have to tell you, two things happened.

The amount of money we were paying for Part A went way down as a percentage increase; and hospitals changed in America. They are still in the process of change. There is no question about that.

The important part of it though was because we put a price on a service we changed the way in which those services were delivered all over this country. I would hope that we all keep in mind that the key to getting costs under control is change the way we deliver services.

You went through a beautiful illustration just a bit ago talking about cardiograms. If we can change the way we are doing this sort of thing, we are going to get those costs under control. There is no question about it. And we means the people. It does not mean the Federal Government, the State Government or anyone else.

Medical markets as I have observed them are strictly local markets. The fact that we talk about Minnesota does not mean Minnesota is the only one that is in it. If it were not for Fargo, North Dakota, Grand Forks, North Dakota, Sioux Falls, South Dakota, the Mayo Clinic being able to get all over the country, we would not have this kind of change.

So it is not a question of whose State is better than anybody else, but you need to look—we all need to look at Minnesota, Utah, Hawaii, Oregon, places like that. I mean, Ube Reinhart jokingly says, you know, when a doctor in Florida wants to take a vacation he just does more procedures on a patient and that means that a doctor up in Deluth cannot go skiing up in northern Minnesota. That is the way the current system operates.

Medicare pays our doctors $274 a month on the average and pays doctors in Miami something like six hundred and some bucks to do the very same thing to the very same people.

The CHAIRMAN. How can that be?

Senator DURENBERGER. Well, in the facts, the variation in practice, in the costs of practice, that Medicare will reimburse in America, from one County, the lowest cost County, to the highest cost County in America is 300 percent. The actual cost of practice difference is in the neighborhood of 16 percent.

The only point I am trying to make—I am not trying to attack universal coverage, because I think that is a critical objective. I am trying to make sure we all acknowledge that the key to getting costs under control is changing the system. And the issue really is, how do we see it happening in our States now. There are a lot of changes going on.

But you are here this week to tell us—this is my interpretation, tell me I am wrong—you said it is in your power to give this change some direction, you at the Federal level, with your reimbursement systems, with your insurance systems, with a whole lot of other things, with your tax systems, with your Medicare, with your low income, with all that.

You are in a position at the Federal level to give it some direction. And if you do not give it some direction we are left with no choice other than to do it at our level.

Governor CHILES. But if you do it and you micro manage it again, no matter what changes you make, they will get unraveled.

Senator DURENBERGER. Right.

Governor CHILES. Now if you allow us to do it with some flexibility and in a market driven system, then I think you will see some real change.

Senator DURENBERGER. Well, let me just take on what I think are the three elements and get to the third one, system reform. The system has got to change. Does anybody disagree with that in one way or another?

Governor DEAN. I absolutely agree with that. I think you can look to your own State to see what you have done in Minnesota, which is a remarkable record. I think it is because we have moved towards what you might called managed care, capitated care, with this different system. DRG's were a great thing because they paid by diagnosis not by the number of procedures. But now, of course, the response to DRG's is computer gaming so that you get the highest possible one.

So I think the next steps beyond DRG's frankly is to get as much of the Medicaid and Medicare population and everybody else's population——

Senator DURENBERGER. Into health plans.

Governor DEAN [continuing]. Into health plans. I maintain they have been criticized because there is loss of choice of doctor. In fact, the opposite is true. And under the Clinton approach and I am sure some of these other approaches, because you have to offer more than one plan to your employer, there is actually more choice of physician not less.

But if we do not get these people into health plans, we are never going to control the costs without a huge bureaucracy, which I agree with Lawton, ultimately is going to fail.

Senator DURENBERGER. Well, before my time runs out, let me see if I can just establish the three things that we really ought to be spending some attention to. One is system reform. And whether we just set the national rules and let the markets work, which is what I believe we do in Cooper, Cooper, Cooper, Cooper, Breaux and Durenberger and Grandy.

Somebody had to make it bipartisan. The system has to change, you know. Secondly, insurance reform. Everybody has agreed on that. Instead of letting it be a state-by-state deal we are going to have national rules now for accountable health plans or whatever it is and that they are going to be implemented at the local level.

But the third one we have in here today is coverage reform. There is not a lot of coverage reform in the Clinton proposal. They proposed to give $60 billion away in drug benefits to the elderly who are already covered; $80 billion in early retiree to people who are already covered. They do not reform the Medicare system so that all of the elderly can buy health plans in your community and those health plans can begin to buy long term care services for people.

The low income issue that we talked about earlier needs to be dealt with at this level. And the change in the Tax Code is also important. I leave it because I have to leave. But the other part of this issue is the debate over long term care.

I have a proposal that just says we should take over the acute care like Reagan proposed in 1982 and we almost did the deal, which would have saved you a lot of money.

We will just take the long term care money that currently exists, put it in a block grant and you decide how to spend it. Then we are going to have to pay some attention to tax policy, savings policy, all the rest of that sort of stuff so that people are not spending down to put people into nursing homes and things like that.

The only point being, there are a lot of challenges in this committee if we are willing to do coverage reform on our way to universal coverage. The way we reform the social insurance subsidy, the tax subsidy and stuff like that, today with these 1950's models and 1960's models, is really critical to solving the problem of universal coverage.

The CHAIRMAN. Governor Campbell, you wanted to say something.

Senator DURENBERGER. Yes, I am sorry.

Governor CAMPBELL. Senator, yes. There are a couple of questions that you asked that I think are important. Howard Dean answered a question on capitated services. There are several problems as we move toward capitated care relating to tort reform. If people demand a service or ask for a service, and are turned down and something happens, you are increasing the liability of the attending physician.

Under the Clinton plan a person would sue the health alliance. So that really needs to be addressed in it.

The other thing that nobody has talked about here is, there is no first party discipline in the insurance system. Everybody has somebody else to pay. I have a card, a Medicaid card or this kind of card. Everybody wants to just go in and get it. They overuse the system because it is "free" and their insurance company is going to pay for it or somebody else is going to pay or I have already paid for it and, therefore, I am going to use it.

We have to in any system we put in, in any system we put in, there has got to be some first party discipline built into it if you are going to have any economic disincentive to overuse the system. I urge you to include some first party responsibility regardless of what you adopt because I believe that it will go a long way towards maintaining some equilibrium throughout the system.

I even think on a capitated payment that the individual ought to have to pay a co—payment for coming to the doctor, a very minor co-payment. People have to understand that it costs money.

The CHAIRMAN. Let the record show that Governor Dean nodded.

Governor DEAN. I am agreeing with Governor Campbell, Mr. Chairman.

The CHAIRMAN. And our last questioner. Senator Chafee has been so generous. May I say to the Governors, I have to address the Legislative Council of the American Association of Retired Persons. If you will excuse me, with my great gratitude on behalf of the whole committee, Senator Packwood will preside and we will say as much for all of us when that time comes.

Governor CAMPBELL. Thank you, Senator.

The CHAIRMAN. Senator Chafee.

Senator CHAFEE. Thank you, Mr. Chairman. First, before you leave, Mr. Chairman, the Medicaid managed care provision without the Federal waiver that they were talking about comes from the Moynihan bill.

The CHAIRMAN. Thank you.

Senator CHAFEE. So you can share in the glory.

The CHAIRMAN. We will all share in this glory. You heard Senator Dole say so.

Senator CHAFEE. Everybody nods. You are for that.

Governor DEAN. Yes, Senator.

Governor CAMPBELL. Yes.

Governor CHILES. Yes.

Governor LEAVITT. Yes.

Senator CHAFEE. When you were talking, Governor Campbell, about individual responsibility in the capitated payment system; in essence you were talking about a co—payment of some kind.

Governor CAMPBELL. Yes,sir.

Senator CHAFEE. I must say I was very pleased in reading what the Governors' Association endorsed, that you come out with what we call the tax cap. In other words, you arrive at—how you get there I am not sure, but you arrive at what is a reasonable cost of a benefit package.

Anything above that, that the employer provides, is nondeductible to the employer and is taxable to the employee, right?

Governor CAMPBELL. Yes.

Senator CHAFEE. Yes. Right Lawton?

Governor CHILES. Yes.

Governor LEAVITT. Yes.

Governor CAMPBELL. We did not come out for denying people to buy other insurance that was not tax deductible.

Senator CHAFEE. No, no.

Governor CAMPBELL. They can buy up what they want.

Senator CHAFEE. And if you get something beyond the benefit package, what we call supplemental benefits, that of course, is nondeductible by the employer and nondeductible by the employee; or taxed.

Governor CAMPBELL. Yes.

Senator CHAFEE. I presume that all of you, when you are talking about some people falling through the cracks and there has to be a public health entity out there to take care of them, that you are talking community health centers to a good degree, right?

Governor CAMPBELL. Most of us have them, yes, sir.

Senator CHAFEE. Yes. And I presume they have worked well with you. I am a big fan of community health centers.

Governor DEAN. Yes.

Governor CAMPBELL. Yes.

Governor CHILES. Yes.

Governor LEAVITT. Yes.

Senator CHAFEE. Now I must say that every day brings home to me the importance of these reforms that are not unique to our bill. I just saw yesterday in connection with a provision we have the antitrust reforms. Maybe you saw the two hospitals in Pueblo, Colorado who wanted to combine.

I believe my figures are not totally accurate but roughly, that they have a combined bed capacity of 560 and they have a combined bed occupancy of 160. And the FTC voted five to nothing, forbidding them to merge. So that gives us, I hope, some impetuous to do——

Governor CAMPBELL. Senator, I do not think that is the exception either. I think that is more the rule of what we have run into in trying to get some of these things done.

Governor LEAVITT. And if you would like examples I bet all of us could provide them.

Senator CHAFEE. I bet. Well, if you want to send in some examples we would appreciate that. There are some, not on this committee, but certainly in the Senate, that think this is just a mirage. This business about the need for antitrust reform and where we are trying for mergers would result in cost increases is single minded. I think probably what is going to happen in Pueblo is one of the hospitals will fold and you will still end up with only one hospital.

Governor LEAVITT. Senator, we have in our State two of our major hospitals, one is a State University owned facility and another is a nonprofit hospital. They have spent the last nearly 3 years now engaged in defending themselves against an antitrust investigation, which appears now to be wrapping up with no findings. It has cost literally millions of dollars and has prohibited them from any kind of progress.

The two hospitals were actually even—well, it is a long and painful story. But there are very good examples out there where this is clearly standing in the way of important reform.

Senator CHAFEE. Well, I could not agree with you more. If we in the Congress came up with a health care plan that incorporated many of the things you ask, maybe not all—as Governor Chiles mentioned, it is a wish list—but let us say you do not get it all; how many of the States do you think would embark on their own plan? I am not going to pin you down.

Governor CAMPBELL. I think most of them would because most of us are already trying to do some things at the State level to different degrees—from a Minnesota and a Hawaii that are underway to those of us that have major waivers pending. I think most of the States are already out there trying to move. I could not say that all of them are.

Senator CHAFEE. Do you find many of your States troubled by mandates that your legislatures have imposed, maybe over your vetos or before you got their mandated benefits? Is that a problem?

Governor DEAN. It is a problem Senator. That is one of the reasons the Governors in our policy asked for a federally mandated benefit package. We hope it will be reasonable, of course. But we believe the benefits ought to be consistent from State-to-State and totally portable. The only way that can happen is if the Federal Government decides what the benefit package will be.

I might also add we are on record as supporting an antitrust legislation because of the problems that you have underlined.

Senator CHAFEE. Now in our legislation we have a very strong medical liability reform provision. It is far stronger than the administration's, which is just sort of try out alternative dispute resolution; whereas we get right in there and put pain and suffering caps. We have caps on percentages lawyers can take and contingency fees. We have only half of the punitive damages go to the Plaintiff; the other half goes to the States to have a retraining fund.

But the biggest single problem I had with what you are suggesting is the exemptions from ERISA. I abbreviate that because you do not put aside all of ERISA, but you wish some exemption from ERISA.

We have had a lot of people come in and see us, obviously multi-State operations, that find that proposal just provides them with chaos.

Let me just give you an interesting statistic. We had a meeting with a national retailer, who is in not all 50 States, but I presume 40 States. He told me a startling statistic—this, Mr. Chairman—they have 60,000 jobs in his company—60,000—and they send out 225,000 W–2 forms a year. That was startling to me. That nearly is four occupants per job. By job I mean a full-time equivalent.

I can understand that getting the exemption from ERISA, you want to have a payroll tax or a tax on health benefits. That is what they are worried about. They are worried about two things.

One, they are worried about the differences that arise in their requirements in 50 States and what that means to them in trying to handle this, and what it means to their employees as their employees move around the country and end up in different plans.

The second thing, and there is no concealing it, is they think you are probably going to come up with what they consider to be a secret tax, one that the public does not know about, on health insurance premiums.

Governor DEAN. Senator, let me try to respond to that. I am sure that Governor Campbell is going to want to respond to this as well. I think, frankly, that the concern among those large international or national companies is misplaced and exaggerated, to be just very blunt about it. The National Governors' Association has asked for a Federal benefits package. So any employee in any State would be in the same plan because the benefits would be the same across States.

That preserves the problem that ERISA addressed originally, that you had to have different mandates in different States about mental health or alcohol counseling or whatever. So that, in fact, insulates them from that problem.

On the second issue in terms of costs, we need an ERISA waiver because unless the Federal Government designs the way this is going to be funded, an employer mandate or what have you, we are going to have to fund this ourselves and we are moving in that direction now.

The reason we need an ERISA waiver is exactly the reason that you said. Not so much for a payroll tax because I do not think any of us are thinking of a payroll tax.

Senator CHAFEE. I should not have said payroll tax, I mean a premium tax.

Governor DEAN. A premium tax. Many of us are considering premium taxes. We are not. I am not in Vermont, but there are those who are. The reason they are doing that is because there is a cost shift now. I believe some of these companies expect us simply to raise taxpayers' costs so high to eliminate the cost shift in health care reform. We cannot do that. We cannot afford to do that.

Most of the international and national companies that I have talked to understand that they are going to continue to pay some sort of a cost shift because the only alternative is the unthinkable possibility of raising taxes by 25 percent and giving those businesses a tremendous break in their bottom line.

So the companies that I have talked to are willing to be flexible about the question of an ERISA waiver. They clearly do not want to have 50 different benefit packages in 50 different States. The Governors do not call for that. But we are clearly going to need some flexibility under ERISA unless the Federal Government does go with an employer mandate and we do not agree that that is—I mean, some of us believe that is a good way to do it and others do not.

That is why the ERISA piece is in there so that Minnesota can go with their premium tax; so that Vermont can have an employer mandate which some people believe is illegal under ERISA; so that South Carolina may use a different mechanism, yet a different one.

Senator CHAFEE. Well, I am glad that you are having success in persuading those companies that your plan is all right. I might refer some of the people who come to see me to you.

Governor LEAVITT. Senator, until I was granted the privilege of this public service by the people of my State I was running a company that had an ERISA plan and we covered employees in four States. Might I add that I would have grave concern about any complete elimination of that opportunity.

I mean it solved problems for us that would have been enormous had we had to deal with individual plans and individual circumstances in all of the States where we do business.

However, I think there are ways and a middle ground in which this can be solved. The problems I was dealing with then and the ones I am dealing with now can both be solved.

I do have a problem in our State now as we move toward passing a pre-existing condition law or a guaranteed insurability law or any of the other reforms in that I cannot impose those now as a State on roughly 70 percent of the employees in my State. Therefore, I am without capacity to make those changes on an effective basis.

So that is one area where on an optional basis the Congress could allow States the option or compelling them to make that part of their plan. It is very limited. It is a very narrow area. But you give us the option. I would be the first to stand and say we should not as States be given unlimited capacity to tax those plans.

On the other hand, it is possible that you could give us a ban of authority in which we could operate so that control clearly stayed with the Congress, but it would give States the capacity to do some things that are very important, in which those plans clearly benefit.

I described earlier a problem we have on some quality matters. Like Senator Durenberger, we have a major research institution, medical search. All of the people in our State benefit from the doctors and the physicians that are trained and we have grave concerns as to where they fit in. It is not inconceivable at some point in time that that financing mechanism may need to be part of it. We would not argue for unlimited capacity to access them. But potentially on some ban given on an optional basis.

Governor CAMPBELL. Senator, could I just expand a little on what Governor Leavitt was talking about. I am not seeking an authority to tax. I do not want an authority to tax. I do think there are some things we need to understand though.

That is that, if we are going to have a Federal minimum benefit package as Governor Dean said, we do not have any ability to know whether ERISA plans to comply to or not. We do not know whether we are going to pick up something that is not covered by an ERISA plan in our public system or our high risk pools.

I think we just have to take these things into consideration as we move forward. I think ERISA is necessary. I think it is absolutely essential for us to have this mechanism to go nationwide.

By the same token, Governor Leavitt has made I think some very good points, that there are going to be circumstances, and you can narrowly define them, that we are going to have to be able to coordinate, at least with what companies are offering under an ERISA plan in order to be able to function in our States.

Senator CHAFEE. This is my last comment, Senator, and I appreciate your staying. Our bill requires the States to impose these insurance reforms on all companies, in other words the pre-existing condition and not turning people down and so forth. So under our legislation we do not exempt ERISA plans from that.

That particular problem, those 70 percent would not be exempt from those.

Governor LEAVITT. That goes a long way.

Governor CAMPBELL. That goes a long way toward what we are doing. And even though the Governors call for a tax cap that is equal across the country if you are going to have one—and I will say that again. If you are going to cap anybody as far as a tax cap for a policy—self-employed, big companies, little companies, anybody else—it ought to apply equally.

Senator CHAFEE. You mean multi-State companies?

Governor CAMPBELL. Anything you are going to cap for deductibility purposes into a plan ought to be equal.

Senator CHAFEE. Nationwide.

Governor CAMPBELL. No, you are going to have to look at the cost area and have a formula for a cost in an area and growth built into it for such things as inflation. But it has to apply equally. You cannot tell some people they can have 100 percent deductibility for the best plan that money can buy and somebody else that you cannot have it except for a portable plan.

Senator CHAFEE. I am not sure we could do this Nationally. For example, let us just say for the sake of argument that the costs of medical care in New York State are higher than the costs of medical care in Utah. So under our plan let us say that you take the average cost of the lowest 50 percent plans that were presented in the health care area, let us say it is a State. So you might well end up obviously with the average—I mean the reasonable costs for a plan to achieve this average is higher in New York State than in Utah.

And yet that is the basis from which you determine whether the plan that is given to you by your employer is a portion of it taxable or——

Governor CAMPBELL. I do not think you can do one size fits all on the country on this, Senator.

Senator CHAFEE. No. But you were just saying within that area you have to treat everybody the same.

Governor CAMPBELL. Right. What I am going to say is, if you are considering a tax cap, that it has to be equitable. And any such cap as that would recognize differences in costs in regions and things of that nature and inflation.

What I am really driving at is that if you exempt certain employees and certain groups from the tax cap, then it is not equitable. That is the only point I wanted to make.

Senator CHAFEE. Our tax cap applies to those companies under ERISA.

Governor DEAN. We think it ought to apply to everybody.

Senator CHAFEE. It would. Our plan does. It does not exempt the ERISA company.

Governor DEAN. We agree with you, Senator.

Senator CHAFEE. All right. Thank you.

Senator PACKWOOD. I want to ask just Governor Leavitt one question and then the rest of you one, and then you will be out of here in 5 minutes.

Governor Leavitt, on page 4 of your statement I read what I think you mean is an income redistribution statement. "A Federal income transfer is required to provide universal access for the uninsured. This transfer is an income redistribution that provides subsidies to those over the poverty level who do not have enough income to purchase health insurance. Without a subsidy program those just under the poverty level have no incentive to increase their income because of the complete loss of health coverage through Medicaid. This is an appropriate role for the Federal Government because the State does not have a sufficient tax base to make the income redistribution required."

Do I read it correctly?

Governor LEAVITT. I know of no plan that when you get into the last 3 or 4 percent will not require some form of Federal involvement. I see no way——

Senator PACKWOOD. You mean taxing the rich to pay for the subsidy for the poor if I read the statement correctly.

Governor LEAVITT. Well, if you look at all health care you could boil it down to one statement. You are taking from those who have and giving to those who do not have.

Senator PACKWOOD. All right. Now, let me just ask the rest of the Governors, and this is this variance thing that I do not quite grasp yet. Earlier, Governor Dean, you said maybe we are better off to take on the trial lawyers one big step at the national level instead of 50 times around and we pass something big and leave it to the States to do within our cap or whatever we do. I understand what you are saying.

But I want to now take specific plans. Oregon's Medicaid waiver can function only because there are certain mandated things that the Federal Medicaid law requires, that they are going to allow us not to do under this waiver.

Let us say you have a national plan and one of the benefits is the payment for chiropractic. And you all know the debates in your State. You, Governor Dean, you probably doubly know the problem. Let us say we pass it and it costs Vermont $20 million a year to reimburse chiropractors. And you say we can use that money better for physical exams for people over 55, the same amount, $20 million.

Should you have the power to vary that kind of a benefit?

Governor DEAN. The position of the NGA, and I think it is a position I agree with, is that I would be willing to give up that power if I could have more control over how many alliances we were going to have or how the physician—patient relationship was going to be allowed to hopefully continue without too much bureaucratic interference, how much capitated or managed care I could use as opposed to being required to have a fee-for-service, so I guess the position of the Governor is, we ought to have a national benefit package that is portable.

If you tell me that chiropractors are going to be included, as a medical doctor and as a Governor, I will accept that. If you say we are going to include this benefit package and it is going to cost us $20 million, you are going to get some resistance from me because the way the Clinton package is structured, there is a maintenance of effort and then additional things like that that we believe as Governors you ought to pay for, if you are going to tell us you are going to do them.

But we believe there ought to be a federally structured benefit package, which is not too rich and not too poor, and that in general I think, although I am not sure it is an NGA policy—I believe all four of us would agree—that the individuals have to pay something as well because there has to be that——

Senator PACKWOOD. I do not quarrel. I agree with you. And I think it frankly ought to be more than 20 percent. But do you all agree that if we have a national benefit package the States should not be able to vary the benefits? You can vary the delivery system, but should not be able to vary the benefits.

Governor DEAN. We should not be able to mandate additional benefits, but we should allow individuals in any State to buy more coverage if they want.

Senator PACKWOOD. But you should not be able to drop benefits in exchange for something you regard is more valuable on another benefit.

Governor CHILES. It would not be portable.

Senator PACKWOOD. I agree. And it would not be a national health plan.

Governor DEAN. That is correct. We agree with that, Senator.

Senator PACKWOOD. Governor Campbell?

Governor CAMPBELL. The portable part of it is what we are talking about. We would not exclude anybody from buying any other coverage they wanted in any location in America. I think we would be foolish of any of us to think that we can design a plan that fits everybody. If people want to buy more, additional coverage, that is fine.

What we are looking at is whether we have the portability and with the transient population that we have in the country it is absolutely essential and there has to be some basic definition of this portable policy.

Senator PACKWOOD. Here is what I want to make sure, because it comes back to Oregon and the Medicaid waiver. We are now going to provide a level of benefits different than the national mandate so that we can experiment with it.

I think you are saying we should not be allowed to do that. We can provide more, but we should not be allowed to drop any benefits.

Governor DEAN. Senator, we are actually saying two things. I thought about this when Senator Chafee was questioning about ERISA. One of the reasons we have taken this particular position on ERISA and it is as strong as it is, is because in the absence of Federal legislation or if the bill were to be passed tomorrow and nothing will happen until 1999, we are ready to go now.

So ERISA prevents us from doing anything. We can enact a plan and I believe we will enact a plan at the end of May in Vermont that will get everybody covered by January of 1995. It is not going anywhere without some sort of an ERISA waiver.

But as the plan progresses, we probably need less waiver. Now the benefits, Oregon needs the waiver and I supported the Oregon waiver, even though we would not use that system in Vermont, because the Federal system is so much of a mess.

You did it because you do not have enough money to do what you think you ought to do, which is the right thing, which is to cover more people for the same amount of money. All of us, I think, vigorously supported Oregon's waiver for just that reason.

But if the system were to work properly, you would never have needed an Oregon waiver because everyone would have been covered with a decent benefit package and you would not have had to make those kinds of choices.

Governor CAMPBELL. Senator, there is one thing, and Senator Chafee said it awhile ago, on ERISA. My concern is not to tear up ERISA and tear up companies or go to the tax side. My concern is that if we are going to have a minimum portable policy out there that we want to make sure that whatever that policy is is met at a minimum under ERISA. That has to do with delivery systems in your States.

Senator PACKWOOD. Fellows, thank you very much. It has been an extraordinarily worthwhile morning. I appreciate your patience in staying with us.

The hearing is adjourned.

[Whereupon, at 12:55 p.m., the hearing was adjourned.]

APPENDIX

Additional Material Submitted

Prepared Statement of Governor Carroll A. Campbell, Jr.

Good morning Mr. Chairman and members of the committee. We appreciate the opportunity to appear before you today on behalf of the nation's Governors to discuss state perspectives on health care reform.

In this statement, we would like to discuss several major issues as follows:

- the Governors' health care reform policy;
- the appropriate state role in health care reform;
- health care spending among states;
- the importance of waivers in health care reform; and
- pursuant to your request, briefly offer you our perspectives on the strengths and weaknesses of four plans to reform our nation's health care system that are before Congress this session.

THE GOVERNORS' HEALTH CARE REFORM POLICY

Health care reform continues to be a major priority for both NGA and individual Governors. Earlier this week, NGA had its winter meeting here in Washington. Health reform was a major topic. Governors remain convinced that changes to the American health care system are needed. This again is reflected in some new statements adopted by Governors that outline a minimum set of reforms. However, before discussing that package, we would like to take a moment to set the context for our perspectives on health reform.

Over the last several years, we have pursued health care reform policy on two tracks. The first calls for the enactment of a comprehensive federal framework with state flexibility and the second calls for immediate enactment of those federal legislative changes that are necessary to allow states to move now to effectively reorganize the delivery system, increase access, and restrain costs. Taken together, these two complementary tracks form a cohesive and comprehensive state perspective that must be considered by Congress and the administration as you approach health reform.

In February 1993, the Governors adopted a comprehensive policy on national health reform that calls for universal access to affordable quality health care. The policy supports a national health care system that recognizes the importance of a federal framework for health reform, but at the same time, recognizes the essential roles and responsibilities of states. The Governors' framework is inclusive of managed competition and would guarantee universal access. It would include: a core national benefits package that is tax deductible; an emphasis on primary and preventive care; insurance reforms that address guaranteed renewability, portability, and availability; limits on the tax deductibility of insurance premiums, tort reform; antitrust changes; administrative simplifications; and the development of national health outcomes so that Americans can assess the quality of their health care. The policy allows for purchasing cooperatives at the state level but does not specify that they should be mandatory or voluntary and there are differences of opinion among Governors on this issue.

The Governors believe that strong cost control systems are integral to any health care reform system adopted for the nation, but effective cost control can be achieved only in conjunction with universal access. As a group, Governors do not endorse enforceable budgets, preferring budget targets instead. We reasoned that setting enforceable budgets for one-seventh of the American economy requires, at a minimum, a stable and objective national data system that does not now exist. And, finally, the Governors call for major reform of the Medicaid program so that all current Medicaid recipients could receive their acute care coverage in a managed care setting.

Our second track addresses a number of reforms that must be pursued now. Those reforms include permitting states to implement Medicaid managed care programs through state plan amendments as opposed to waivers, and the establishment a waiver process for ERISA so that states have the opportunity to implement broad-based financing mechanisms for state reform and to include self-insured plans in state-based reform programs. Managed care for the acute care portion of Medicaid will help recipients get appropriate prevention-oriented care. This will increase the quality of care in the Medicaid program, help to control costs, and provide a medical home for beneficiaries who historically have had trouble finding reliable care. I will speak more directly to the issue of waivers later in my testimony.

A Call For Action

By the end of our first meeting last weekend, we realized that despite differences on employer mandates, global budgets and mandatory alliances, there was a great deal of common ground among us about strategies to address many of the nation's health care problems. Also, we agreed that those strategies must be addressed this year. Governors became convinced that we would contribute most to the national debate by adopting policy which reflects our consensus position. Therefore, last Monday, we adopted a policy statement that calls upon President Clinton and Congress to pass health care legislation this year that includes, at a minimum, the following:

- insurance reform;
- state-organized purchasing cooperatives;
- core benefits and access;
- limited tax deductibility of health care premiums;
- low income subsidies;
- changes to the current Medicaid system;
- medical malpractice and liability reform;
- relief from anti-trust statutes;
- relief from the Employee Retirement Income Security Act;
- federally organized outcome and quality standards; and
- administrative simplifications.

We believe that these provisions should be included in any reform strategy. As Governors, we do not vary in our support of these changes, and we urge Congress and the President to act as quickly as possible.

HEALTH CARE SPENDING AMONG STATES AND HEALTH CARE REFORM

Mr. Chairman, you have asked us to address the extent to which federal health care reform should seek to reduce a variety of health care spending disparities among states. The disparity to which you refer is most salient in the state and federally funded Medicaid program. Major disparity results from the Medicaid matching formula. Determined by federal statute, a state's contribution to the cost of services is based on its per-capita income compared to the national per-capita income. Disparities among states also result from differences in the number of optional Medicaid health care services that a state chooses to provide. States differ in the amount, duration and scope of any particular service, and finally, they differ in reimbursement rates. Aside from the matching formula and differences among states in the demand for high cost/high volume services for which no financing adjustments are made, these differences are reflective of state policy choices and are consistent with the state/federal partnership of the program.

The Medicaid matching formula and the differences among state Medicaid programs takes on special significance in the President's Health Security Act because state Medicaid spending is the basis for the maintenance of effort provisions that will help fund the plan. Our membership has taken no position on the equity of the Medicaid matching formula, and Governors do not agree on the need to make changes.

Mr. Chairman, you have also asked us to address the extent to which federal health reform proposals should have a redistributive effect among individuals. Governors have endorsed policy that supports a limitation on the variation in insurance rates that different individuals and groups could be charged. We understand that this policy could have a redistributive effect among individuals. However, we also support limitations on medical underwriting, guaranteed renewability, and portability of health insurance. In addition, we support a variety of other actions that would lower the overall cost of health care. So, while limitations on the variation in rates might have a redistributive effect, the overall result should be beneficial to all.

And finally, Mr. Chairman, you asked us to address the extent to which states are willing to be accountable for health care expenditures and cost containment within a federal framework. There is no simple answer to this question because it is so dependent upon the specifics of the health reform proposal.

Our willingness to be accountable for health care expenditures within a federal framework is dependent on the extent to which the health care reform proposal funds care to those populations currently covered by states. Within the context of the Clinton plan, we have said that states' contribution should be no greater than Medicaid expenditures that would be supplanted by the national program. However, some states have been more aggressive in both the breadth of their benefits package and eligible populations who are covered. They should not be penalized for attempting to use the Medicaid program so extensively to provide services. Second, we would urge you to be cautious in reducing the disproportionate share hospital program as a source of funds. Under any reform strategy, some subset of people living in the U.S. will remain uninsured, and states must have some federal assistance in paying for these people. In any case, we believe that some state-by-state negotiation will be required in determining state contributions to a new health care system.

Our willingness to participate in cost containment within a federal framework will require significant consultation among the Governors. Our policy does not support a budget cap; however, if one is to be imposed we would like to work closely with Congress and the administration to assure that the strategies are equitable and workable.

WAIVERS AND INCREMENTAL HEALTH REFORM

The growing demand for affordable quality health care coupled with the immediate budgetary pressures caused by the Medicaid program requires immediate action on reform, and virtually every Governor has some health initiative in progress. They range from comprehensive state based reform initiatives, to programs that assist small businesses in securing affordable health insurance, to expanding health care coverage to a greater number of uninsured poor, to implementing managed care networks for Medicaid beneficiaries. None of these state initiatives are incompatible with national reform; instead, they continue to build a strong policy foundation for reform at the federal level. State innovation through waivers must not be constrained because of the debate on national health care reform; instead, it must be encouraged as an essential way to facilitate a health care network infrastructure as a way to encourage states to begin to deal with the most difficult of problems—comprehensive network-based care for special populations.

Medicaid Managed Care Waivers

The private sector has led a national trend in health care service delivery toward systems of care. These systems or networks have been shown to provide cost efficient care while assuring the patient a medical home—a reliable place to seek primary care and from which specialty care can be directed. Yet, as the private sector is moving aggressively toward these networks, the Medicaid program continues to require states, in virtually all cases, to apply for a waiver from fee-for-service care in order to enroll Medicaid beneficiaries in such networks. And while the Bush and Clinton administrations have taken significant steps toward simplifying the application and renewal process, states still must re-apply for renewals every two years. Moreover, states have been unable to sustain networks where there is a predominance of Medicaid beneficiaries because under current law; states are permitted only one non-renewable three-year waiver to have beneficiaries served in a health maintenance organization (HMO) where more than 75 percent of the enrollees in the HMO are Medicaid beneficiaries. This requirement should be. repealed.

If the nation is serious about controlling health care costs, giving states the opportunity to establish networks in Medicaid, including fully and partially capitated systems, through the regular plan amendment process is essential to achieve this goal. Governors recognize the special significance of consumer protections and assurance of solvency in establishing these systems of care and support federal oversight through the regulatory process.

Comprehensive Waivers

Many states have begun to look seriously at comprehensive systems of health care where the artificial categorical barriers of Medicaid are removed and where states can establish statewide networks of care for Medicaid beneficiaries. These strategies are being developed in response to the fact that with efficient cost containment, states may be able to deliver health care to a greater number of poor people. Unfortunately, there are no provisions in the Social Security Act that give states any certainty that these networks, once established, can remain a part of the state's health care delivery structure.

Currently, states have been developing these more comprehensive network through the research and demonstration provisions of the Social Security Act (Section 1115a). Because Section 1115a was designed for research purposes, it has some important limitations. States must demonstrate through the application process that they are testing an innovation. The law requires an evaluation that in some cases requires control groups. Projects approved under the 1115a process are approved for a limited time period, usually three to five years at the discretion of the administration, and require special statutory changes to go beyond the demonstration period. Finally, these projects must be cost neutral over the life of the project.

Section 1115a is essential to allow the testing of alternative health and social policies. However, the current statute falls short by requiring statutory changes if a state wants to continue its successful effort. In short, once a state has proven that its research project works, it cannot continue without Congressional action. Governors support changes to the Social Security Act so that a state may apply through the executive branch of government for renewable waivers of their innovations. This waiver process should be consistent with the streamlined approaches used by the Clinton administration and states should have to reapply for these waivers no less than every five years.

Employee Retirement Income Security Act Modifications

While the Governors are extremely sensitive to the concerns of large multistate employers, the fact remains that one of the greatest barriers to reform initiatives that some states wish to pursue is the Employee Retirement Income Security Act (ERISA). ERISA preempts all self-insured health plans from state regulations and subjects those plans only to federal authority. As a result of judicial interpretations of ERISA, states are prohibited from:

- establishing minimum guaranteed benefits packages for all employers;
- developing standard data collection systems applicable to all state health plans;
- developing uniform administrative processes including standardized claims forms;
- establishing all payer rate setting systems;
- establishing a statewide employer mandate;
- imposing premium taxes on self-insured plans; and
- imposing provider taxes where the tax is interpreted as a form of discrimination against self-insured plans.

Governors call on the administration and Congress to modify the ERISA statute to give states the flexibility they need to move ahead on a variety of approaches to health reform. This may be done either by establishing the flexibility directly in statute or through the establishment of waiver authority. The flexibility could include a requirement that the state demonstrate broad-based support for the change, such as by passage of state legislation. States must be assured, however, that the flexibility is stable and not unreasonably time limited.

STRENGTHS AND WEAKNESSES OF HEALTH CARE REFORM PROPOSALS

Mr. Chairman, we would like to discuss briefly, some of the strengths and weaknesses of four health reform plans that are before Congress this session. Those plans are the President Clinton's Health Security Act, Senator Breaux's Managed Competition Act, Senator Chafee's Health Equity and Access Reform Today Act, and Senator Nickles' Consumer Choice Health Security Act. For the sake of brevity, we will refer to the proposals by their author.

It should be noted that current Governors' policy has not considered the overall strategy of totally replacing the business tax exclusion of company sponsored health plans with individual tax credits that is the basis of the Nickles proposal. As such, the collective view of the Governors is unknown. Also, while there is significant agreement among the Governors on aspects of national health reform, we do have three areas of disagreement including whether there is a need for an employer mandate, whether alliances should be voluntary or mandatory, and whether there is a need for enforceable budgets. As such, our comments are bounded by policy adopted by the nation's Governors through the National Governors' Association.

Alliances/Purchasing Cooperatives/Health Care Coverage Areas

The Governors support an approach to national health reform that includes alliances or purchasing cooperatives. We believe that states should have flexibility in establishing and operating alliances within a national framework, and we support a flexible governance structure that could allow for public or private administration under state regulation. Governors disagree about whether alliances should be mandatory or voluntary.

The Clinton, Breaux, and Chafee proposals all call for the establishment of alliances. Where the Clinton and Breaux proposals establish mandatory alliances, the Chafee proposal establishes voluntary health care coverage areas (HCCAs) with voluntary purchasing groups. We strongly believe that states should have some choice as to how the alliances/purchasing cooperatives would be governed. This perspective is reflected in both the Clinton and Chafee proposals. However, the Clinton proposal gives the national health board significant authority to the point that it is unclear whether state governance structures will have any meaningful responsibilities.

States should have some flexibility to determine the best method for governing alliances be it a branch of government or a private non-profit organization. Breaux offers no flexibility to states regarding governance. Clinton and Chafee do. As we support flexibility in alliance governance, we also support flexibility in drawing alliance boundaries, including statistical metropolitan areas. Neither Clinton nor Breaux allow states to subdivide these areas. We believe that such flexibility gives us the opportunity to encourage plans to cover rural areas by drawing boundaries that would link rural areas to more favorable suburban and urban areas. Of the three, only the Chafee proposal gives states that flexibility. Finally, unlike Breaux where the national board certifies health plans, both the Chafee and Clinton proposals give that responsibility to states.

If national reform includes alliances or purchasing cooperatives, we urge you to resist the temptation to give both states and the federal government regulatory authority over these entities. Instead, we encourage you to give the states regulatory authority while reserving for the federal government oversight of state responsibilities. This will give states and these entities the clarity that they need to operate efficiently and effectively.

Cost Containment

Governors' policy does not support the Clinton cost containment strategy of enforceable budgets. We believe that, in the short run, there are insufficient reliable data upon which to base such an important policy decision with such significant implications for the nation. Although the cap is determined and enforced at the federal level, the impact on states is direct. If the federal government fails to set reasonable limits in the first several years, states may be left with the responsibility for correcting the damage done to providers, networks, and the availability of care.

NGA policy supports the limit on tax deductibility of heath insurance premiums that are included in the Clinton, Breaux and Chafee proposals. NGA policy, however, calls for immediate imposition of that limitation, not a delayed or phased in approach.

The Governors strongly oppose the cap on Medicaid expenditures of both the Chafee and Nickles proposals. We believe that this establishes an artificial barrier on a program that has seen extensive growth in the last several years. With such a cap, states would have to assume the full burden of care when federal funds were exhausted. It is true that both proposals support a per-capita federal cap that allows for changes in program growth; however, neither addresses the fact that Medicaid has an individual entitlement to care with a range of mandatory eligibility groups and services. Their strategy simply limits the financial exposure of the federal government at the expense of states.

Medicaid and Low-Income Programs

Governors consider changes and modifications to the Medicaid program to be one of the most important aspects of health care reform. Except for the Breaux proposal that makes a wholesale swap of acute care and long-term care between states and the federal government, each of the other proposals takes an incremental approach to change.

Clinton/Chafee/Nickles. Looking narrowly at Medicaid, the Clinton proposals are generally consistent with Governors' policy. Medicaid acute care services would be integrated into the same delivery system used by all Americans. This unitary acute care service delivery structure should dramatically reduce the incentive for a two-tiered health care system that results from our current Medicaid program. In addition, states will have more financial certainty in the growth of their Medicaid budgets because of the limits and predictability of payments for both the cash categorical populations and maintenance of effort for the non-cash categorical populations. These advantages are not trivial.

However, we also have several concerns about the Clinton approach to Medicaid. First, the plan calls for a maintenance of effort payment based on federal fiscal year

1993 expenditures. That payment is trended forward over the transition period until the plan takes effect. Data from states show that the growth in the Medicaid program is abating (and may be as low as 8 percent this year) and it is looking like the administration may have overestimated that projected growth. Therefore, states could be put in the position of expending more money for this maintenance of effort than would have otherwise cost to pay directly for beneficiary care.

Second, states must make payments directly to alliances for beneficiaries in the Aid to Families with Dependent Children (AFDC) and the Supplemental Security Income (SSI) programs. Since the late 1980's Congress has moved to delink Medicaid from cash assistance programs; that is, a person could qualify for Medicaid without participating in either AFDC or SSI. By re-establishing this programmatic link, states will have to consider health care costs as it makes policy decisions about AFDC and SSI. Third, the President's plan gives states relief from the Boren amendment for hospitals but fails to do so for nursing facilities. States must be given some relief so that their program costs can be brought under control. Regarding Boren, Governors support a strategy that would establish reimbursement rate methodology "safe harbors." These safe harbors would give states predictability in expenditures and protections from costly law suits.

Aside from its arbitrary cap on Medicaid expenditures the Chafee proposal makes incremental changes in Medicaid that Governors have long requested. Specifically, the states will be able to establish both risk based and non-risk based managed care systems in the Medicaid program without waivers. And while the Chafee proposal maintains a separate Medicaid program outside of its purchasing cooperative system, states are given the option to phase-in selected Medicaid beneficiaries for their acute care services with certain protections.

The Nickles proposal establishes new broad waiver authority under Medicaid in which states can pursue alternative cost effective health care. But the program would be required to operate under a problematic Medicaid cap.

The Breaux proposal takes a bold step by having the federal government assume the cost of acute care services while having the states assume the costs of long-term care. It has been said that this swap is favorable to states as evidenced by a Congressional Budget Office (CBO) analysis. However, we believe the analysis is flawed because it assumes that only a subset of services that have traditionally been considered long-term care would be given to states. If Congress chose to give states all the other traditional long-term care services, as seems likely, the swap would be much less favorable. In addition, CBO, in its estimates, did not model the fact that the nation will age over the next couple of decades. An aging population will require proportionally more long- term care at proportionally more costs. NGA policy actually supports a swap where the states assume acute care and the federal government assumes long- term care.

Of the four proposals, only the Clinton proposal would significantly modify long-term care services. While we cannot support the new unfunded mandate to require states to establish a medically needy program for long-term institutional care, we support in principle, the new optional program for community-based long-term care. We remain concerned that although this new program is not an individual entitlement to care, the courts may interpret it as such. Such a judicial interpretation would have a devastating effect on state budgets, and might force states that would have otherwise supported this optional program to choose not to offer it to their citizens.

CONCLUSION

Mr. Chairman, we have tried to give you the state perspective on a broad range of issues regarding health care reform. We know that you and the members of Congress have an exceedingly difficult task ahead of you as you begin your deliberations. We would like to leave you with several thoughts.

First, states have been important incubators for emerging national public policy. Please do not lose sight of the wealth of information that is available to you from state health care experiments of the last decade or allow states to be stymied in their efforts to move ahead on reform while Congress deliberates.

Second, once the debates are over and legislation is passed here in Washington, it is the states who will have responsibility to administer the program. This is appropriate. However, please do not bind us with excessive regulation and structure. Give us the flexibility so that we can create a workable program in each of our states without the need from the outset to return to Congress for minor changes. The overly prescriptive nature of Medicaid should be held up as an example of what not to do.

Finally, states have an immediate need for some latitude to do experimentation. Title 11 of the Social Security Act, by example, has a provision that allows states the opportunity to conduct health and welfare research and demonstration projects. Governors believe that this provision was added to the Act because Congress recognized that good social policy is alive, vibrant, and dynamic and that policy must be malleable in response to the changing American landscape. That idea must be kept alive and incorporated in your final product.

Thank you for the opportunity to appear before you today.

Prepared Statement of Governor Lawton Chiles

I would like to thank the members of the Finance Committee for inviting me to testify today on state perspectives in health care reform.

There is no one single issue with wider impact than health care. It is bankrupting families, hurting small businesses, causing painful cuts in state budgets and adding demonstrably to the federal deficit. Several states, including Florida, have moved to address this crisis.

The states have found it difficult, however, to test health reforms because they are subject to many strict and unyielding federal laws and regulations. Franklin Roosevelt once said that "practically all the things we've done in the federal government are like things Al Smith did as governor of New York," underscoring that many of the New Deal social programs, including Social Security and unemployment compensation, were modeled on successful state programs. The widespread retreat from federalism and greater use of peremptory federal laws and regulations prevents the federal government from capitalizing on this proven approach to social and health reforms.

The social programs of the 1960s included a massive federal investment in new health care programs for elderly and low income people and public health funding. The 1970s was a period of rapid technological advancement, continued investment in the nation's health care infrastructure, changes in the commercial insurance market, growth in employer self-funding, and staggering increases in health care expenditures. In the 1980s we saw a period of retrenchment. Spending limits, debt, and entitlement costs forced the federal government to cut block grants, eliminate federal programs and attempt to accomplish its social agenda through state mandates. Greater responsibility for health programming was shifted to the states. Faced with fewer resources and greater mandates, the states in the 1990s have begun implementing comprehensive reforms, including setting universal coverage deadlines, reforming insurance practices, controlling costs, testing managed care and managed competition strategies, and reforming the Medicaid programs that were increasingly consuming states' growth revenues.

Former President Bush set a cooperative tone when he asserted that "innovation at the state level can address the problems of rising medical expenditures and access to quality health care . . . states (should be encouraged) to test new and creative ideas and provide incentives to experiment with new initiatives by allowing states flexibility that is not available under current law." The federal government should renew federalism, eliminating micromanagement of state programs, permitting states to adopt diverse policies that meet the conditions and needs of their citizens, and achieve social and economic objectives through cooperative efforts.

I am greatly encouraged by President Clinton and the First Lady's focus on health care reform. They have established a new era of close consultation and cooperation with the states. The Department of Health and Human Services has approved major federal Medicaid waivers in record time, granting the states the flexibility they need to fully implement their health reforms.

While I believe the federal government should encourage state initiatives to provide full coverage of their citizens and operate cost-effective health care programs, it has a legitimate interest in ensuring that each state will carry out the intent of national objectives. I suggest the following general principles guide decisions on state flexibility:

1. The state's health care reforms must be comprehensive, ensuring access to care for all residents by a certain date;
2. The state must agree to enter into an outcome-based performance contract in exchange for being granted waivers from federal requirements;
3. Benefits must include preventive and primary care in the basic plan design.

FLORIDA'S REFORM EFFORT

As Florida approaches the year 2000, pressing questions about the cost, quality and accessibility of health care overshadow nearly all other concerns and threaten the economic and social well-being of the states. Florida has one of the nation's largest uninsured populations. Nationally, only three other states—Alaska, New Mexico, and Texas—exceeds Florida's rate of uninsurance for those ineligible for Medicare. Nearly 23 percent of those below the age of 65 are uninsured, representing over 2.5 million residents, about one third of whom are children. Over 82 percent of uninsured Floridians have incomes below 250 percent of the poverty level; almost 700,000 have incomes below the poverty level but are ineligible for Medicaid.

The majority of the uninsured reside in families where there is a full-time worker. Approximately 75 percent are in families in which the head of the family or their spouse work at least 17.5 hours per week. Almost 52 percent work for firms with less than 25 employees. About 66 percent work for firms with less than 100 employees. Preliminary data from a Florida survey conducted in the summer of 1993 indicate that nearly half of the state's firms with fewer than 50 employees fail to offer insurance, representing almost one-third of the work force.

Part of Florida's high uninsurance rate can be explained by the characteristics of the states' business community. Large businesses are more likely to offer health insurance as a benefit than small businesses, but 95 percent of Florida's businesses employ fewer than 25 people. About half of all new job openings between now and the year 2000 will be in low paying, service employment positions such as retail sales, cashiers, or food service workers. These positions are among the least likely to offer health insurance as an employment benefit.

For employers, health benefit expenditures are rising faster than wages, salaries, and profits. Unless we act now, the cost of health benefits could overtake wage and salary increases by the turn of the century. This shows how unsustainable our current health care system has become.

Through Medicaid, Medicare and the growth of employment based insurance coverage, large numbers of Americans receive their health care through some kind of third party arrangement. While such a system is effective in paying their bills, it does little to develop cost conscious consumers or providers. Many recipients and providers alike view today's health care coverages as virtually free—"my insurance will cover it." In truth, however, the national cost of health care has skyrocketed from $1 billion each month in 1950 to more than $2 billion every day. Efforts to contain costs have been largely unsuccessful; instead they have simply shifted costs from one resource to another. Federal responsibilities shift to the states; states draw ever more stringent eligibility guidelines; providers shift uncompensated care costs to insured patients; insurance companies raise premiums; and businesses pass along their increased costs to their consumers.

In Florida, as in the rest of the U.S., overall health care costs far exceed general inflation. For a family of four, 100 percent of the 1993 federal poverty level means an annual income of $14,350. If a family at the poverty line was able to purchase health insurance at the average Florida premium for conventional, employer-sponsored coverage, the cost of the insurance would represent at least 32 percent of their annual income—and the family would still be responsible for deductibles and copayments. The same coverage would represent 13 percent of the income of a family of four at 250 percent of the 1993 poverty level.

The United States currently spends more for health care than any other nation, yet the average life expectancy is shorter and the infant mortality rate is higher than those of other industrialized countries. Despite numerous improvements in publicly-sponsored health programs and significant increases in health-related expenditures, Florida ranks lowest among states in overall indicators of residents' health.

Through Medicaid expansion, the Healthy Start initiative, health promotion and personnel deployment programs, Florida has improved its health status ratings. However, much remains to be done. The statistics are chilling:

- Every four hours a baby dies in Florida.
- In 1991, more than 193,000 babies were born in Florida—almost 2,000 did not reach their first birthday.
- Florida ranks sixth in the number of teenage pregnancies. In 1991, 13.8 percent of all births were to mothers under age 20.
- Every 35 minutes a low birth weight baby is born in Florida.
- Approximately 10,000 babies were born each year test positive for cocaine or other drugs.

With the nation's "oldest" population, it is natural that Florida would rank near the top among states in death rates for many common diseases and conditions—but there are other indicators of health status that affect younger people as well.

- Every day seven Floridians die from breast cancer. The overall cancer death rate has increased every year since 1979.
- Florida ranks third nationally in the total number of AIDS cases, and second in the number of pediatric cases.
- Florida's violent teen death rate is the seventh highest in the nation.
- About one in six Florida deaths is directly attributable to smoking.

In a system such as ours, where a majority of people have health insurance coverage it is often difficult to explain why the need for health care reform is so critical. More and more Floridians, however, are finding their access to basic health services severely limited by their inability to purchase affordable coverage. Even people who have insurance are not immune. Just when they need it most, many Floridians find that the health insurance they thought would protect them from financial ruin is a safety net full of holes. For government, commitments to fund increasingly expensive health care programs leave less revenue to fund other critical needs, such as education, public safety and the environment. For businesses, rising health care costs contribute to a decreased ability to compete in the global marketplace, as prices are continually boosted to cover higher employee benefit costs. With such a large portion of revenues being diverted to health benefits, less capital is available for research and development or long-term investment.

The consensus for change is growing. Health care providers, insurers, consumers, purchasers, and government are calling for better, more workable ways of providing and paying for quality health care. These same people are calling for more accountability in the health care system—including a higher level of purchaser and consumer data to help inform decisions that will bring a new level of discipline to the marketplace.

In 1991 we began with a goal that every Floridian should have access to comprehensive, affordable health care. Over the last three years we have moved assuredly toward securing a healthy home for all Floridians. I believe we have found the workable solution for Florida.

The Health Care Reform Act of 1992 set an ambitious goal—December 31, 1994—to achieve universal coverage and a mandate for a public/private partnership to achieve it. While we knew that achieving this goal would be difficult, we were encouraged that a bold standard would convert our best intentions into tangible results. Next, we passed a comprehensive reform law that will ensure that every Floridian receives coverage at a community rate.

In 1993, the Florida Legislature enacted the Health Care and Insurance Reform Act of 1993. That act established the framework for a voluntary, market-based managed competition through 11 Community Health Purchasing Alliances and provider networks. Florida's reforms do not mandate employers and individuals to purchase health insurance, employers to contribute to the cost of health insurance or employers to join our Community Health Purchasing Alliances.

The managed competition health care model is based on the assumption that provider groups, health insurers, and managed care companies must assume responsibility for the kind of internal restructuring that is crucial to what will become the new competitive bottom line in health care: public accountability for health care's impact on patient satisfaction, function and well-being, all at reasonable costs. Under such a plan providers and insurers must voluntarily design and promote a common approach to laying the foundation for the next generation system of health care.

The 1993 legislation also mandated additional small group reforms, major new health care information systems, the development of practice parameters, and the further consolidation of health care programs, including Medicaid, in a single health care financing, planning, purchasing, and regulatory agency.

For 18 months, Florida has been riding the fast track towards health care reform. In this short period, we have:

- Enacted the Health Care Reform Act of 1992;
- Created a single state agency for health care planning, policy, purchasing, financing, and regulation in July, 1992;
- Published a comprehensive reform plan, the interim Florida Health Plan A Blueprint for Health Security, in December 1992;
- Enacted the Health Care and Insurance Reform Act of 1993 in April, 1993;
- Established 11 Community Health Purchasing Alliances in October, 1993;

- Published the final Florida Health Plan in December 1993: The Florida Health Security Plan: Healthy Homes 1994;
- Established its managed competition model, establishing 11 Community Health Purchasing Alliances, directed by boards of 17 members;
- Developed a rural health network development program and awarded contracts for the development of four rural health networks in December, 1993;
- Designated Accountable Health Partnerships;
- Issued the small employer group health insurance RFP in December, 1993 (the first AHP bids are due February 10, 1994);
- Reduced the rate of annual growth in the Medicaid program by more than 50 percent in the last year;
- Established an initial set of practice parameters in December 1993;
- Implemented joint venture reforms in 1992 and 1993.

Already there are solid signs we are succeeding: insurance and health care cost increases are slowing down; more efficient networks of providers are beginning to compete on quality and price; quality managed care programs are taking hold; and our citizens are accepting more responsibility for their health.

FLORIDA HEALTH SECURITY—A SECTION 1115 MEDICAID DEMONSTRATION PROGRAM

Florida has identified several problems with federal Medicaid statutes and regulations that prevent the states from ensuring access to health care for all their citizens, operating cost-effective programs, and implementing other comprehensive health care reforms. State efforts to cover additional low income, unemployed or part-time workers, implement wide scale managed care programs, and demonstrate other cost containment measures have been limited by Medicaid categorical and income limits, the linkage of federally supported public and medical assistance eligibility, managed care limitations, and federal financial participation restrictions.

Florida Health Security, a bold new public-private partnership, ensuring low-cost, high quality health care coverages for uninsured, working Floridians. It will also build on the managed competition model currently being implemented in Florida through the 11 Community Health Purchasing Alliances allowing employers to provide coverage to employees and their dependents in a voluntary market.

Florida Health Security will:

- Provide discounts for individual and employer premium costs, ensuring very affordable health coverages;
- Provide an attractive benefit package that includes broad inpatient, outpatient, primary care, preventive care, prescribed drug, mental health and substance abuse, and some long-term care and community-based services;
- Provide coverage to 1.1 million uninsured Floridians; and
- Utilize a market-based, regionalized purchasing system administered through the Community Health Purchasing Alliances.

Florida Health Security is federal and state budget neutral. No new taxes will be required. The program will provide premium discounts for individual/employee and employer premium costs. Individuals and families with incomes below 250% of the federal poverty level (82% of Florida's uninsured population), who are U.S. or documented persons and Florida residents are eligible. The program will use a simplified eligibility process.

Employers and individuals insured within last 12 months will be ineligible for Florida Health Security. Entire families, however, that have had one or more family members continuously uninsured for 12 months may join the program. Employers will not be required to participate in the program, contribute to the cost of employee premiums, or enroll employees not eligible for premium discounts.

The program would implement significant Medicaid reforms including: (1) mandating managed care for all Medicaid recipients; (2) implementing reimbursement reforms that limit annual program expenditures to caseload growth + CPI + plus points (2.9 points declining to 0 over several years); (3) reallocating hospital disproportionate share program funds; (4) eliminating the medically needy program; and (5) potentially reallocating funds from other federal, state, and local funds that provide direct patient care because of the lack of insurance coverages.

Many Floridians from all walks have taken an interest in our health reforms and have participated in hundreds of public meetings over the last 18 months. Our future success depends on federal flexibility and consumers and purchasers who are well enough informed to begin to deal more economically with health care payers and providers.

Our reform proposals are intended to bring health care into the bright light of the information age and get a message of greater personal responsibility and active participation to all our state's residents. We believe that there are many solutions to our problems. The real answers will be worked out at the local level in natural health care market regions. There is much to be done, and a role for every level of government to play.

PREPARED STATEMENT OF GOVERNOR MICHAEL O. LEAVITT

Good morning Mr. Chairman and members of the committee. I appreciate the opportunity to appear before you today to discuss a state's perspective on health care reform. In this statement, I would like to address the following two topics:

1. Utah's plan for health care reform.
2. Federal flexibility required to implement Utah's plan.

UTAH'S PLAN FOR HEALTH CARE REFORM

Last week I presented to the Utah Legislature my plan for reform of the state's health care system. *Utah Healthprint—a Blueprint for Market-Oriented Health Care* is a process that will lead to increased access to affordable insurance coverage for all Utahns. This state-based solution is tailored to address the unique needs and culture of individuals in Utah. This uniqueness is evident in the basic decisions I made in formulating this plan and in the plan itself.

Basic Decisions

The first question I had to answer was whether the employer or individual should be responsible for health care coverage? I feel that the individual has the primary responsibility for their own health care coverage. This decision does not change the incentives employers currently have to provide coverage for their employees, but it clearly indicates that employer mandates do not foster the business climate we want in Utah.

The second question was whether we should fix the market or create a government-run system? In many of Utah's health care market segments, competition is alive and well. I opted, therefore, to address the problems in the current marketplace rather than to overhaul the whole system. I do not believe in government-run health care.

The third question was whether the state should implement comprehensive reform all at once (a big bang approach) or follow a master plan (or blueprint) that directs us to a target? I chose a blueprint approach for reforming health care, which accounts for one-seventh of the state' economy. The big bang theory of health care reform makes hundreds of complex decisions all at once and then fixes unanticipated problems later. A flexible master plan does not lock the state into untried solutions, but directs us to our target of increased access to affordable insurance coverage. The blueprint approach recognizes that health system reform is a long-term, ongoing process.

The fourth question was what level of choice should consumers have in choosing health plans and doctors? We know that unlimited choice increases costs and restrictions lower costs. I determined that the level of choice should be decided by the consumer. To the degree the consumer wants to save money in purchasing health insurance, they will accept restrictions. In cases where the state is providing coverage, it should have the ability to direct the individuals into the most efficient health care delivery systems.

The final basic question was how increased access should be financed? The four typical methods to finance reform, in order of preference, are: (1) savings, or doing more with what you have; (2) higher insurance premiums; (3) general taxes; and, (4) cost shifting. All four methods will likely continue to finance health care for some time. However, current public sentiment prohibits using new taxes as a method to expand access in Utah.

The Plan

The answers to these questions are the underlying principles for *Utah Healthprint*. Healthprint is a flexible master plan to increase access to affordable health care coverage, contain costs, and maintain and enhance quality. It anticipates that the Utah Legislature will debate and enact reforms each year. The state must take a significant first step in 1994 to commit itself to the target and reform process. A health policy commission, chaired by the governor, will provide a mechanism for the sustained effort and leadership that this process requires.

Access

Healthprint recommends the following four strategies to increase access:

1. Insurance reform
2. Medicaid expansion
3. A Co-op
4. Federal income transfer

Insurance reforms will increase access for many individuals who are excluded in today's marketplace. For example, guaranteed renewability would mean that insurers could not cancel or refuse to renew coverage of a health insurance policy except for failure of the insured to meet contractual obligations, such as non-payment of premiums. Portability of insurance can be achieved by requiring insurers to waive preexisting conditions and accept anyone who changes from one insurance plan to another. Through a modified community rating, wide variations in premiums can be reduced while maintaining incentives for healthy lifestyles. Insurance reforms address the need of many Utahns for health coverage security.

Medicaid expansion will allow the state to cover all residents living below the poverty level. By using the most preferable method of financing access, for example, doing more with what you have, the state will expand access through savings in the Medicaid program. These savings accrue when Medicaid recipients receive coverage in capitated, managed care settings. Let me emphasize that access will be expanded only when actual savings are realized. This financing method is consistent with the fiscally conservative way the state of Utah is managed.

A buying co-op will address the problems of access in the individual and small employer market. Individuals and small employers commonly lack access because insurance premiums are simply unaffordable. A co-op will pool individuals and small groups of less than 50 to allow them the same administrative economies of scale that large companies experience when purchasing health benefits. A co-op will also allow increased choice for employees working in small companies. Currently, many who work for small employers have a choice of only one health plan. Through a co-op, a choice of many different plans will be made available to them.

A federal income transfer is required to provide universal access for the uninsured. This transfer is an income redistribution that provides subsidies to those over the poverty level who do not have enough income to purchase health insurance. Without a subsidy program, those just under the poverty level have no incentive to increase their income because of the complete loss of health coverage through Medicaid. This is an appropriate role for the federal government because the state does not have a sufficient tax base to make the income redistribution required for the subsidy.

Cost Containment & Quality

Medical costs are escalating at a rate that Utah cannot afford. Costs will be contained by enhanced competition through a co-op and a greater use of capitation. Quality will be maintained and enhanced through competition rather than a government-mandated top down approach.

A co-op promotes price and quality competition among health plans by giving individuals information needed to make intelligent, cost-conscious choices. One of these choices could be a medical savings account, a concept supported by many in my state. Increased consumer involvement in the purchasing of health care is absolutely necessary if costs are to be contained. Capitation, as a reimbursement method, will likely increase as vertically integrated health plans compete. Alternatives to capitation will be necessary in the rural areas of the state.

Quality of care must not diminish as health system reform is undertaken. As competition is enhanced, plans will not only compete on price but will also be evaluated on quality. Providers of care have an essential role in recognizing needed improvements, designing improvement strategies, and carrying out improvement projects. The most effective improvements will occur when energy is devoted to systematically identifying and improving specific, targeted care processes rather than through compliance to government standards.

FEDERAL FLEXIBILITY REQUIRED TO IMPLEMENT UTAH'S PLAN

Utah cannot successfully implement our plan for health care reform without receiving flexibility from the federal government. For *Utah Healthprint* to be successful, changes need to occur in the following three areas:

1. Employee Retirement Income Security Act (ERISA)
2. Medicaid Requirements
3. Federal Income Tax Law

ERISA

A major strategy to expand access is through insurance reform. The state, however, cannot apply insurance reforms uniformly for all its residents. ERISA exempts self-insured companies from state laws that affect health care benefits. Utah seeks limited changes to ERISA to implement reforms consistently for all residents. For example, portability of insurance is achieved by requiring insurers to waive preexisting conditions and accept anyone who changes from one insurance plan to another. However, if an employee changes jobs from an employer with a state-regulated plan to an employer with an ERISA plan, the ERISA plan could impose preexisting conditions. Additionally, as the state narrows the variation in health insurance premiums through our modified community rating, estimates show that 21 percent of our state-regulated companies would opt to become ERISA plans. This flight of good risks from the state-regulated market would dramatically inflate premiums for those under the community rate and undermine the intent of the reforms.

The quality improvement effort under this reform plan will require funds to build data systems for quality measurement. Consumers need to be given information to compare the quality between health plans. We have considered a nominal surcharge on health insurance premiums to fund the quality measurement system. However, under current interpretations by the courts, this surcharge could not be applied to ERISA plans, even though they too would benefit from the quality data.

Medicaid Requirements

Current Medicaid statute and regulations hamper Utah's ability to implement effective cost containment programs. Elimination of federal barriers would ensure a productive partnership between Utah and the federal government in expanding access to the uninsured and containing cost in the Medicaid program. These barriers exist in three areas: (1) Medicaid eligibility; (2) client responsibility; and (3) managed care.

In the area of Medicaid eligibility, Utah needs, first, the ability to eliminate the Medicaid categorical requirements—i.e. aged, blind, disabled, Aid to Families with Dependent Children (AFDC)—to design our programs around family financial characteristics. A key strategy in *Utah Healthprint* is to expand Medicaid to cover all individuals below the federal poverty level and not limit coverage to those who fit a defined category. Second, the state needs the flexibility to define the family unit. Currently, different definitions for a family unit are used depending on whether eligibility is based on AFDC or Supplemental Security Income (SSI) regulations. As a result, extensive confusion and litigation surround this issue and make it difficult for the state to structure our plan. Third, the Health Care Financing Administration has made it impractical for a state to apply more liberal eligibility methodologies allowed under Section 1902(r)(2) of the Social Security Act. Under a Section 1902(r)(2) option, the state could eliminate the linkage to AFDC and SSI and adopt a uniform income standard applicable to the entire Medicaid population. Flexibility in these three areas would strengthen Utah's ability to tailor the Medicaid program to cover our low-income population.

Client responsibility is absolutely necessary to contain costs in Medicaid. States have little flexibility in developing effective methods for requiring clients to use Medicaid services appropriately. Specifically, cost sharing may be levied on only a very small proportion of Medicaid clients. In addition, the cost sharing amount allowed is too nominal to be effective, too difficult to administer, and cannot be required in some instances. Utah needs the flexibility to design a cost sharing program that extends to all Medicaid clients. For example, the state should be given the option to charge cost share payments to the following month's AFDC grant for cash recipients. Additionally, the state should be given the option of requiring the co-payment before non-emergency services are provided Options to include incentive programs as well as cost sharing should also be permitted.

Cost-effective managed care program implementation, such as HMO contracting, should be allowed through a simple State Plan amendment. Currently, states are required every two years to obtain and renew Freedom of Choice waivers to implement managed care programs. States with these waivers have demonstrated the value of managed care programs over the past ten years. Therefore, Utah recommends eliminating the requirement for states to obtain and renew Freedom of Choice waivers every two years.

Federal Income Tax Law

Federal tax policy has created our employment-based method of providing health insurance. The state plan will correct the inequity experienced by individuals who do not have employer-provided insurance through changes in the state income tax law. Affordability of health insurance would increase if a similar change were made at the federal level, providing a financial incentive for this typically uninsured group to purchase coverage. Additionally, medical savings accounts need the same tax treatment as health insurance plans to be a viable alternative to managed care as a cost containment tool.

CONCLUSION

Utah is actively pursuing a state-based solution for reform of our health care system. Health system reform is a long-term, ongoing process. The unique needs of my state will be addressed best through our master plan for reform. I believe that *Utah Healthprint,* with flexibility granted at the federal level, will direct my state to our target of affordable access to health insurance.

UTAH *Health*PRINT

"A Blueprint for Market-Oriented Health Care"

A BLUEPRINT FOR MARKET-ORIENTED HEALTH CARE

At the request of Governor Leavitt, the 1993 Utah Legislature established the Health Care Policy Option Commission to propose options for reforming the state's health care system. The commission completed its work and issued a final report in December 1993. The Governor has reviewed the health care reform options recommended by the commission and now introduces Utah Healthprint -- a blueprint for market-oriented health care. Healthprint establishes a rational process for providing affordable health care coverage for all Utahns.

The Target

Utah Healthprint will increase access to affordable insurance coverage for all Utahns. Individuals will not be turned down by health insurers because of a preexisting condition. Employees will not be locked into a job for fear of losing their health insurance. Healthprint will change the rules of the marketplace in order to provide the security of health care coverage for all Utahns.

The spiraling rise in health care costs will be contained through enhanced competition. Through increased consumer involvement and a change in provider incentives, the health care market would have increased price competition--a proven method of cost control.

The high level of quality health care enjoyed by Utahns will be maintained. In fact, the quality of care will increase as providers make continuous improvements required by a competitive environment.

The enactment of Healthprint will begin true health care reform in Utah. Many health reform plans look good on paper but never get tried. Healthprint is a politically feasible solution because it provides a reasonable process for reforming the health care system.

Environmental Assumptions

In developing Healthprint, six major environmental assumptions were recognized and considered.

- Change will occur whether or not the state does anything. Through action, the state can influence the direction of the changes.
- The federal government plays a major role in health care reform whether we like it or not. A national plan could completely undo our state effort. Even without a national plan, exemptions and waivers are required from the federal government to implement state reforms.
- Because the current health care market is in flux, the reform process must be flexible and adaptive to change.

- The state is limited in its ability to address all the complex issues of health care in a 45-day legislative session. At the national level, tremendous resources have been devoted to the health care debate; it could span several years.

- Although they sound good, many of the recommended solutions are untried. The health reform process must allow testing of proposals and flexibility to change direction if they do not work.

- Health system reform will take sustained effort and leadership. The Governor is committed to lead the health care reform effort and keep the state moving toward its target of increased access to affordable care.

Basic Strategy

The basic strategy of Utah Healthprint is to define a flexible master plan. This master plan is a blueprint of the many decisions that need to be made. Annual decision points will occur each 45-day legislative session. The Utah Legislature would debate and enact reforms each year to bring the state closer to target. The state should take a major first step forward in 1994 to commit itself to the target and reform process. A mechanism to make the process succeed is the creation of the Utah Health Policy Commission. As chair of the Commission, the Governor would work with legislators and other appointed members to study health system issues in the flexible master plan and make recommendations for each legislative session. The Commission would also recommend changes to the flexible master plan as shifts occur in the health care environment. Figure 1 illustrates this basic strategy.

Figure 1
Basic Strategy of Utah Healthprint

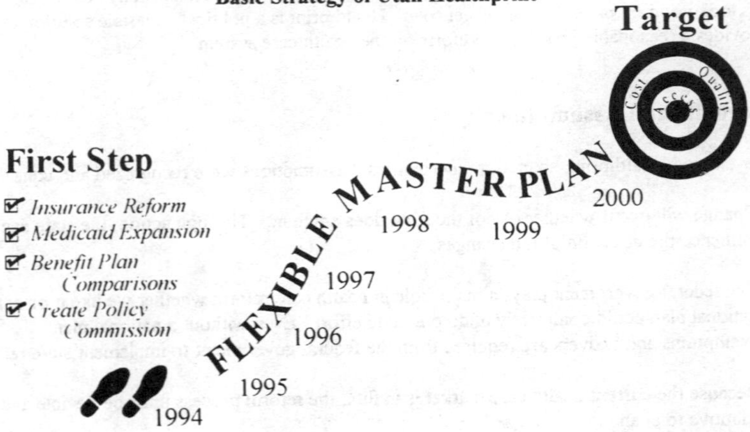

Basic Decisions

In formulating the flexible master plan, the following five basic questions had to be answered:

1. Should the employer or individual be responsible for coverage?

2. Should we fix the market or create a government-run system?

3. Should we implement comprehensive reform all at once (big bang) or follow a master plan (blueprint) that directs us to a target?

4. What level of choice should consumers have?

5. How do we pay for increased access?

These questions were answered as follows:

1. Individuals should be responsible for their own health coverage.

2. We should fix the problems in the current market by enhancing competition rather than setting up a government-run system.

3. We should avoid the "big bang" theory of health care reform, which makes hundreds of complex decisions all at once. A flexible plan is a more reasonable approach than being locked into untried solutions.

4. The level of choice should be decided by the consumer purchasing the health care. We know that unlimited choice increases costs and restrictions lower costs. The consumer is most able to make this cost-conscious decision.

5. The four basic methods to finance reform, in order of preference, are: 1) savings, or doing more with what we have; 2) higher insurance premiums; 3) general taxes; and, 4) cost shifting. All four methods will likely continue to finance health care for some time. However, no new taxes are required to implement Healthprint.

Flexible Master Plan

The flexible master plan addresses the goals of access, cost containment, and quality. This blueprint contains today's ideas for reforming the health care system. The blueprint is flexible and expected to change as new information is available and as transformations take place in the health care market.

Access

The three main strategies to increase access are: 1) insurance reform, 2) Medicaid expansion, and 3) creation of a co-op. The federal government would need to be involved to allow the state to achieve universal coverage. Currently, 89 percent of Utahns have either public or private health insurance. Figure 2 illustrates the plan for expanding access to all Utahns.

Figure 2
Access Plans for the Uninsured

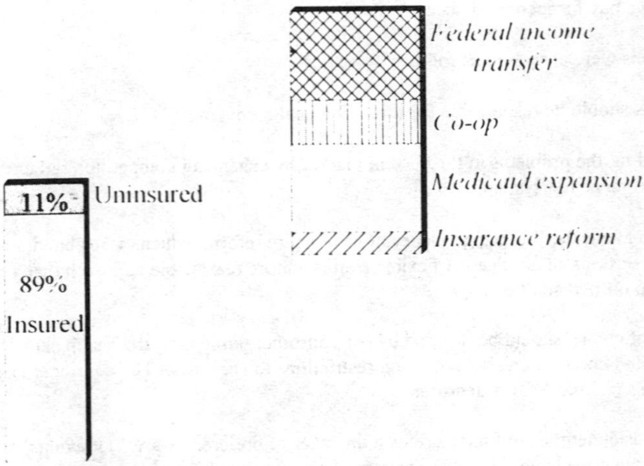

Insurance Reform

The following insurance reforms would take place in 1994 as a part of a major "first step":

- Insurers would provide dependent coverage up to age 26. Many college students who qualify as dependents do not have health insurance. This reform would require an insurance company to include them in the health plan.

- Premiums would be community rated for small groups, allowing insurers to vary premiums only on the basis of age, gender, and geography. To promote prevention and healthy lifestyles, insurers may also give individuals discounts for healthy behavior.

- Small groups would receive guaranteed renewability of insurance. Insurers could not cancel or refuse to renew coverage of a health insurance policy except for failure of the insured to meet contractual obligations, such as non-payment of premiums.

Additional insurance reforms would take place over the next few years. For example, insurers could not exclude coverage of any preexisting medical condition for anyone who changes insurance plans. This would allow portability of insurance for individuals changing jobs. Employees would no longer be locked into a job for fear of losing their health coverage because of a preexisting health condition. A slight increase in insurance premiums is expected, initially, as a result of these reforms. Eventually, the increase will be offset by the decline in premiums due to Healthprint's cost containment strategies.

Medicaid Expansion

The second method to increase access is through an expansion of the Medicaid program. Medicaid is a federally-aided program that is operated and administered by states. The program provides medical benefits for certain indigent or low-income persons in need of medical care. For every dollar the state pays, the federal government contributes three dollars. Medicaid would be expanded in the following four phases and would be financed by the savings generated from changing the way the system operates.

- **Phase I** would provide coverage for all children age 11-17 who are living below the federal poverty level. The state health department estimates that this would provide coverage for approximately 32,000 additional children.

- **Phase II** would provide medical coverage to all aged, blind, and disabled individuals below the federal poverty level.

- **Phase III** would expand Medicaid to cover all others below the poverty level. A waiver from the federal government is necessary to allow expansion in phase III.

- **Phase IV** of the Medicaid expansion would be a federal income transfer that subsidizes the insurance premium for those between 100 and 150 percent of the federal poverty level. This is an appropriate role for the federal government because the state does not have a sufficient tax base to finance a subsidy by itself. Universal access cannot be achieved without this federal income transfer.

Phases I through III would be expanded through savings in the Medicaid program. Under the current Medicaid system, recipients can go to any provider, whenever and as often as they like. This blank-check system provides incentives for over utilization of health care services. The new system for Medicaid reimbursement is to provide health care in capitated, managed care settings. "Capitation" is a method of payment for health services in which an individual or provider is paid a fixed dollar amount for each person served, regardless of the actual number or nature of services provided to each person in a set period of time. Capitation is the characteristic payment method used in health maintenance organizations. This places providers at financial risk, rather than the state, and gives providers incentive to keep their members healthy. Limited choice would remain for Medicaid recipients because they could choose which capitated health plan to join. The state has already begun this new method of reimbursement for 20 percent of Medicaid clients and is financing the first phase of the expansion through actual savings. Expansion into the second and third phases would occur as actual savings accrue from the increased use of capitated reimbursement.

Co-op

The co-op is the sponsor for the small group and individual market. Individuals and small employers commonly lack access due to the unaffordability of insurance. The co-op would pool small groups and individuals to allow them to experience the same administrative economies of scale that large companies experience when purchasing health benefits. The co-op would also allow increased choice for employees working in small firms. Currently, many who work for small employers have a choice of only one health plan. Through the co-op, a choice of plans would be made available to employees of small employers. Figure 3 depicts how the co-op would function.

Figure 3
Function of Co-op in Providing Health Care to Individuals and Small Groups

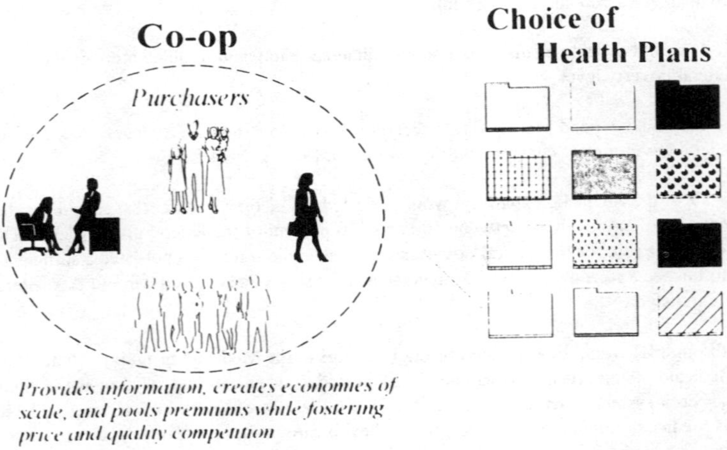

Cost Containment

Medical costs are escalating at a rate that we cannot afford. Utah Healthprint envisions two major elements of cost containment. The first is enhanced competition through the co-op. The second is a greater use of capitation.

The co-op provides a platform for competition. It promotes price and quality competition among health plans by giving individuals information needed to make intelligent, cost-conscious choices. Increased consumer involvement is absolutely necessary as a cost containment tool. Small employers are too small to achieve administrative economies of scale that large corporations experience when purchasing health benefits. Average administrative expense for groups under five people is estimated as high as 40 percent of premium versus 5 percent for groups over 10,000 people. The co-op would provide these economies of scale to individuals and small group purchasers.

Under the co-op framework, use of capitation as a reimbursement method for health plans would increase. Capitation changes the provider's incentive from offering unlimited services to providing services that will promote the health of patients in the long run. It is also likely that medical savings accounts would be offered through the co-op. Medical savings accounts (MSA) allow individuals to purchase a high-deductible policy and put the premium cost differential into a medical savings account to pay for routine medical care. The funds in an MSA would belong to the insured and, if unspent, accumulate over time as savings to pre-fund future health care needs.

Quality

As health system reform is undertaken, quality of care must not diminish. In fact, Utah Healthprint anticipates an increase in quality as health plans not only compete on price but are also measured on quality. Health plans would have incentives to continuously improve their processes to provide improved outcomes for their patients. Under a co-op, consumers would be provided information on patient satisfaction for each health plan. They would also be given information on differences in medical outcomes between health plans.

Quality improvement must occur from the bottom up and not from a government-mandated top down approach. Providers of care have an essential role in recognizing needed improvements, designing improvement strategies, and carrying out improvement projects. The most effective improvements will occur when energy is devoted to systematically identifying and improving specific, targeted care processes. Through such a process, a local hospital was able to reduce the infection rate for major abdominal surgery from 1.8 percent (the acceptable national average was 2 to 4 percent) to 0.4 percent, which increased customer satisfaction, reduced the length of hospital stay, and saved the hospital approximately $750,000 in a single year. This quality improvement paradigm shows that it is possible to increase quality while decreasing costs. The quality approach recommended in Healthprint provides the incentives for such innovations.

UTAH HEALTHPRINT

	1994	1995	1996
ACCESS	Medicaid expansion **(L)** · children ages 11-17 below 100% of poverty Insurance reform **(L)** · cover dependents to age 26 · small group modified community rating · guaranteed renewability Uninsurable risk pool funding increased **(L)** Request federal tax change **(L)** · self-employed and individuals Medicaid waiver application	Medicaid expansion **(L)** · aged, blind, disabled below 100% of poverty Insurance reform **(L)** · preexisting conditions waived Public health plan **(L)** State tax change **(L)** · self-employed Medicaid waiver state approved/forwarded **(L)**	Medicaid expansion **(L)** · adults below 100% of poverty (Medicaid waiver approved) Insurance reform **(L)** · system-wide modified community rating · portability · guaranteed issue · risk adjustment mechanism Special populations plan **(L)** State tax change **(L)** · individuals
COST CONTAINMENT	Administrative simplification Designated benefits offering **(L)** Medicaid capitation · 40% of clients Request federal tax change **(L)** · medical savings account	Electronic submission of claims Self-referral limitations **(L)** Medicaid capitation · 65% of clients Tort reform **(L)** Anti-trust reform **(L)** Healthy lifestyles education **(L)**	Voluntary capitated managed care for companies with <50 employees promoted Medicaid capitation · 100% of clients Co-op created **(L)** · health plans approved · medical savings account option
QUALITY	Practice guideline efforts continued Data systems improved **(L)**	Quality process implementation begins **(L)**	Quality process implementation continued **(L)** Medical education reform **(L)**
STUDY AND EVALUATION	Create Health Policy Commission **(L)** Study items · federal reforms · tort reform · self-referral limitations · anti-trust reform · rural health care · public health · quality process · healthy lifestyles education · medical ethics · access/cost/quality monitoring · insurance reform · state tax equity	Commission evaluation and recommendations · review prior reforms · recommend new reforms Study items · federal reforms · co-op · special populations · rural health care · quality process · medical education reform - primary care - financing education system · insurance reform · state tax equity	Commission evaluation and recommendations · review prior reforms · recommend new reforms Study items · federal reforms · rural health care · alcohol/drug treatment · long-term care · workers comp/auto health insurance · alternatives to capitated reimbursement · benefit plans review

(L) – Legislative action required

1997	1998	1999	2000
Rural health plan **(L)** Alcohol/drug treatment plan **(L)**	Long-term care plan **(L)**	Mental health plan **(L)**	Employer/individual mandate? **(L)** Uninsurable risk pool integrated? **(L)**
Alternatives to capitated reimbursement **(L)** Co-op **(L)** · enrollment for individuals and employers with < 50 employees	Workers comp/auto health insurance integrated **(L)** Public sector co-op? **(L)**	Medicare integrated? **(L)** Medicaid co-op? **(L)**	Co-op **(L)** · enroll employees with 50-100 employees?
Health plan report cards			

Commission evaluation and recommendations
· review prior reforms
· recommend new reforms
 	
Study items
· federal reforms
· mental health
· workers comp/auto health insurance?
· long-term care
· benefit plans review
· public sector co-op?
	Commission evaluation and recommendations
	· review prior reforms
	· recommend new reforms
	
	Study items
	· federal reforms
	· mental health
	· Medicaid co-op?
	· Medicare integrated?
	· benefit plans review
		Commission evaluation and recommendations
		· review prior reforms
		· recommend new reforms
		
		Study items
		· federal reforms
		· co-op
		  - effect on access/cost/quality
		  - include employers with 50-100 employees?
		· employer/individual mandate?
		· uninsurable risk pool?
		· benefit plans review
			Commission evaluation and recommendations
			· review prior reforms
			· recommend new reforms
			
			Study items
			· federal reforms
			· access/cost/quality
			· benefit plans review

EXPLANATION OF HEALTHPRINT TERMS

1994

ACCESS

Medicaid expansion will provide medical coverage to all children under 18 years of age below the poverty level. This expansion will increase the number of children covered by approximately 32,000.

Insurance reform includes:

Dependent coverage to age 26 which will require insurers to offer coverage for all unmarried tax dependents up to age 26;
Small group community rating with modifications for age, gender, and geography. Premium discounts may also be given for healthy lifestyles; and
Guaranteed renewability which will require insurers to renew all policies, unless the employer or insured individual fails to comply with contract requirements such as failure to pay premiums.

Uninsurable risk pool funding increased by $1,500,000. This pool was established in 1990 to provide low cost access to health insurance for those who are denied adequate insurance and are considered uninsurable.

Changes in federal tax law will be requested to allow individuals purchasing insurance the same tax benefit as those who receive health insurance through their employer.

A **Medicaid waiver application** will be written to provide Medicaid coverage for all adults below the poverty level. The expanded coverage will be financed by savings in the Medicaid program.

COST CONTAINMENT

Administrative simplification will create efficiencies in the system. The Utah Health Information Network (UHIN) is a leading organization in the standardization of claim administration practices, electronic data interchange, and the establishment of an information repository.

A **designated benefits offering** will require insurers to quote a price on designated benefits, as well as offer the designated benefit plan to facilitate price comparison.

Medicaid capitation will provide cost savings as clients are moved into prepaid HMO and other managed care arrangements. In 1994, 40 percent of Medicaid recipients will be in a capitated system.

Changes in federal tax law will be requested to allow Medical Savings Accounts comparable tax treatment as other health plans.

QUALITY

Practice guidelines effort will continue through the Effective Practice Patterns Subcommittee which is working on the dissemination of practice guidelines.

Data systems will be improved to provide the information necessary to measure the effectiveness of Utah's health care system. As a first step, additional funding is recommended for the Utah Health Data Committee to begin work on establishing a central data repository.

STUDY AND EVALUATION

A Health Care Commission will be established to study health system issues and recommend additional reforms. This eleven-member commission will be chaired by the Governor. The commission has the responsibility to direct the efforts outlined in Utah Healthprint.

Study items for the commission for 1994 include:

Federal reforms - to monitor federal action and determine its impact on the state;
Tort reform - to study changes in tort law that would reduce defensive medicine;
Self-referral limitations - to study the need for health care professional limitations on self-referral;
Anti-Trust - to determine the need for and actions required for state-action immunity from anti-trust laws for the collaborative use of expensive medical equipment and for the establishment of approved health plans;
Rural health care - to review the most appropriate delivery system for rural areas that will provide access to essential health care services;
Public health - to develop a public health plan that defines standards for public health and recommend improvements to the system;
Quality process - to define a quality system that continuously improves processes and provides appropriate consumer protection;
Healthy lifestyles education - to increase the awareness of healthy lifestyles for Utah residents;
Medical ethics - to determine the method for making ethical medical decisions;
Access/Cost/Quality monitoring - to establish a baseline and process that measures the effects of reform on access, cost, and quality;
Insurance reform - to review the possible elimination of preexisting conditions; and,
State tax equity - to determine how to give self-employed individuals the same treatment for health benefits that employees receive.

1995

ACCESS

Medicaid Expansion would cover all aged, blind, and disabled below the federal poverty level.

Insurance reform would be presented to the legislature and require:

> **Preexisting conditions** to be waived at the initiation of the program. Insurance coverage will have no exclusions or waiting periods on preexisting conditions for continuously covered individuals.

The **public health plan** developed by the Commission would be presented to the legislature.

A **state tax change** would be presented to the legislature and would allow self-employed individuals the same treatment for health benefits that employees receive.

The **Medicaid waiver** to expand access to adults below the poverty level would be presented to the state legislature for approval and forwarded to the United States Department of Health and Human Services.

COST CONTAINMENT

Electronic submission of claims would be implemented statewide. The Utah Health Information Network is developing standards to be used for electronic data interchange.

Self-referral limitations would be presented to the legislature.

Medicaid capitation would provide cost savings as clients are moved into prepaid HMO and other managed care arrangements. In 1995, 65 percent of Medicaid recipients will be in a capitated system.

Tort reform would be presented to the legislature in order to reduce the anxiety of legal action which has produced an environment of defensive medicine in the provider community.

State-action **exemption from anti-trust laws** would be presented to the legislature to encourage collaborative use of expensive medical equipment.

The **healthy lifestyles education** plan developed by the commission would be presented to the legislature.

QUALITY

A system-wide **quality process** would be presented to the legislature and maintain the high level of quality enjoyed by Utah residents. This effort would be phased in over several years.

STUDY AND EVALUATION

Evaluation and recommendations for reforms would be ongoing tasks of the Commission. The Commission would evaluate the effectiveness of prior reforms and recommend new reforms from the items studied during the year.

Study items:

Federal reforms - to monitor federal action and determine its impact on the state;
Co-op - to determine the structure, membership, costs, benefit plans, guidelines for medical savings accounts and health plan approval criteria for the purchasing cooperative construct;
Special populations - to insure access for the homeless, migrant workers, and those who face geographic, cultural, linguistic and physical barriers;
Rural health care - to review the most appropriate delivery system for rural areas that will provide access to essential health care services;
Quality process - to define a quality system that continuously improves processes and provides appropriate consumer protection;
Medical education reform - to increase the number of primary care professionals and determine the financing system for professional medical education;
Insurance reform - to review system-wide modified community rating, portability, and guaranteed issue; and,
State tax equity - to determine how to give individuals the same treatment for health benefits that employees receive.

1996

ACCESS

Medicaid expansion would provide coverage to all adults whose income falls below 100 percent of poverty.

Insurance reform would be presented to the legislature and include:

System-wide modified community rating with modifications for age, gender, and geography. Additionally, discounts to premiums may be given for healthy lifestyles;
Portability which allows an employee who is changing jobs to transfer their insurance and not lose coverage;
Guaranteed issue which requires that all insurers must accept all employer groups or individuals; and,

A **risk adjustment mechanism** required by the likelihood of adverse selection.

A **special populations plan** developed by the Commission would be presented to the legislature. This plan would insure that all citizens with special needs and disabilities are provided access to health care services.

A **state tax change** would be presented to the legislature to allow individuals the same treatment for health benefits that employees receive.

COST CONTAINMENT

Voluntary capitated managed care for companies with greater than 50 employees would be promoted to obtain cost control for groups operating outside the co-op.

Medicaid capitation would reach 100 percent of Medicaid clients in 1996.

A **co-op** option would be presented to the legislature to allow small employers and individuals economies of scale in the health insurance market. The co-op could offer health plans which have met state insurance solvency criteria. One of the health plans could be a medical savings account option, which would allow individuals to purchase a high-deductible policy and put the premium cost differential into a medical savings account.

QUALITY

A system-wide **quality process** would continue to be implemented to maintain the high level of quality enjoyed by Utah residents. This effort would be phased in over several years.

A **medical education reform** plan would be presented to the legislature to produce more primary care providers in Utah including physicians, nurses and other health care professions.

STUDY AND EVALUATION

Evaluation and recommendations for reforms will be ongoing tasks of the Commission. The Commission would evaluate the effectiveness of prior reforms and recommend new reforms from the items studied during the year.

Study items for the commission in 1996 include:

Federal reforms - continue to monitor federal action and determine its impact upon the state;
Rural health care - conclude the review of the most appropriate delivery system for rural areas that will provide access to essential health care services;
Alcohol/drug treatment - to determine the most appropriate system and reimbursement methods for alcohol and drug abuse treatment;

Long-term care - to review the long term care task force recommendations;
Workers compensation/auto health insurance - to determine the feasibility of merging workers compensation and auto health insurance under a single management structure;
Alternatives to capitated reimbursement - to study alternatives to capitated reimbursement systems, particularly in rural areas; and,
Benefit plans review - to review designated benefit plans which facilitate price comparisons.

1997

ACCESS

The **rural health plan** based on the commission's study would be presented to the legislature.

The **alcohol/drug treatment plan** based on the commission's study would be presented to the legislature.

COST CONTAINMENT

Co-op enrollment would be presented to the legislature for final approval and would occur for individuals and employers with fewer than 50 employees, who are purchasing insurance.

Alternatives to capitated reimbursement would be presented to the legislature.

QUALITY

Health plan report cards assessing the quality of care delivered by existing health plans would be published.

STUDY AND EVALUATION

Evaluation and recommendations for reforms will be ongoing tasks of the Commission. The Commission would evaluate the effectiveness of prior reforms and recommend new reforms from the items studied during the year.

Study items for the commission for 1997 include:

Federal reforms - continue to monitor federal action and determine its impact upon the state;
Mental health - to develop a plan to improve the quality and access of mental health care;
Workers comp/auto health insurance - to develop a plan to integrate worker's comp and auto health insurance into a single management structure based upon studies from 1996;
Long term care - to develop the plan for long term care based upon studies from 1996;

Benefit plans review - to review designated benefit plans which facilitate price comparisons; and,
Public sector co-op - to study the need for a public cooperative as described above for private individuals seeking health insurance.

1998

ACCESS

The **long-term care** recommendations would be presented to the legislature.

COST CONTAINMENT

Workers compensation and auto insurance would be presented to the legislature depending on the result of the prior year study.

A **public sector co-op** would be presented to the legislature depending on the results of the prior year study.

STUDY AND EVALUATION

Evaluation and recommendations for reforms will be ongoing tasks of the Commission. The Commission would evaluate the effectiveness of prior reforms and recommend new reforms from the items studied during the year.

Study items of the Commission for 1998 include:

Federal reforms - to monitor federal action and determine its impact on the state;
Mental health - continue review and study of mental health reform implementation;
Medicaid co-op - to study the feasibility and appropriateness of including the non-long term care portion of Medicaid into a co-op;
Evaluate Medicare - to study the feasibility and appropriateness of integrating Medicare into Utah health reform efforts; and,
Benefit plan review - to review designated benefit plans which facilitate price comparisons.

1999

ACCESS

Mental health reforms would be presented to the legislature.

COST CONTAINMENT

Medicare integration would be presented to the legislature depending on the outcome of the feasibility and appropriateness studies.

Enrolling **Medicaid recipients in a co-op** would be presented to the legislature depending on the outcome of the feasibility study. Long-term care would likely be excluded.

STUDY AND EVALUATION

Evaluation and recommendations for reforms will be ongoing tasks of the Commission. The Commission would evaluate the effectiveness of prior reforms and recommend new reforms from the items studied during the year.

Study items of the Commission for 1999 include:

Federal reforms - to monitor federal action and determine its impact on the state;
Co-op - to determine effect, if any, of the co-op on access, cost and quality of health care. Also to assess the feasibility and appropriateness of including employers with 50-100 employees in the purchasing cooperative;
Employer/Individual mandate - to assess accessibility to health care and determine if there is a need for an employer/individual mandate to provide insurance;
Uninsurable Risk Pool - to assess the future need of the uninsurable risk pool; and,
Benefit plan review - to review designated benefit plans which facilitate price comparisons.

2000

ACCESS

Employer/individual insurance mandates would be presented to the legislature if deemed necessary to achieve access goals.

The **uninsurable risk pool** integration would be presented to the legislature depending on the results of the prior year study.

COST CONTAINMENT

Co-op expansion to include employers with 50-100 employees would be presented to the legislature depending on the results of the prior year study.

STUDY AND EVALUATION

Evaluation and recommendations for reforms will be ongoing tasks of the Commission. The Commission would evaluate the effectiveness of prior reforms and recommend new reforms from the items studied during the year.

Study items of the Commission for the year 2000 include:

Federal reforms - to monitor federal action and determine its impact on the state;
Access, cost containment, and quality - to evaluate overall progress in achieving access, cost containment and quality; and,
Benefit plans review - to review designated benefit plans which facilitate price comparisons.

APPENDIX A
QUESTIONS AND ANSWERS ON HEALTHPRINT

1. Why do we need health care reform?

Approximately 200,000 people in Utah are currently uninsured and may lack access to needed health care. Additionally, medical costs are rising at a rate we cannot afford.

2. Does the plan provide universal access to health care?

Increased access to affordable insurance is the goal of Healthprint. The goal is to be achieved over several years as actual savings are realized.

3. What will the proposed health plan do to contain health care costs?

Market forces, increased consumer responsibility, a co-op, administrative savings, capitation, and managed care are major cost containment strategies.

4. Are employers mandated to provide insurance to their employees?

No. The individual is responsible for having health insurance. Financial assistance would be provided eventually for those who are below 150 percent of the poverty level.

5. Is a tax increase necessary to implement Healthprint?

No new taxes are required.

6. Will individuals have a choice of plans or choice of benefits within a plan?

Yes, consumer choice will be preserved and enhanced for individuals and small group purchasers.

7. Will individuals have a choice of provider?

Yes, but the plan anticipates increased use of managed care and capitation. When a consumer joins a managed care plan, provider choices may be limited to those participating in the plan.

8. What if I get sick during one year? Does that mean the insurer can drop my coverage or hike my premiums, like they often do today?

No. Insurance reforms will be implemented over the next few years to preclude this from happening.

9. What is insurance reform?

Refers to the changing of current insurance laws and practices to require such features as guaranteed issue, modified community rating, and portability of insurance from job to job. It may also include prohibitions against preexisting condition exclusions.

10. What is guaranteed issue?

Any person, regardless of age, health condition, etc., will be eligible to purchase a health care plan.

11. What is modified community rating?

A method of calculating health plan premiums allowing modifications in rates for age, gender, and geography. Additionally, discounts to premiums may be given as incentives for healthy lifestyles.

12. What is portability?

Employees can change jobs without losing their health insurance. This eliminates "job lock".

13. Will preexisting conditions be covered?

Yes, after all anticipated insurance reform is implemented.

14. Will my insurance premiums go up?

It depends. They will go up for some and down for others and for many individuals and employers remain the same. They would increase slightly as insurance reforms are implemented but will decline as small businesses benefit from participating in large purchasing pools.

15. What is a co-op?

The co-op is the sponsor for the small group and individual market. The co-op would allow a pooling of risk and reduce the variation in premiums for small groups and individuals. The co-op would increase choice to employees working in small firms with a menu of health plans made available to them. The co-op would give individuals and small groups the same access to benefits plans now enjoyed by employees of large employers.

16. What is the role of agents and brokers?

The role of agents and brokers is likely to change for this market segment. They could operate as benefit consultants to small employers in the enrollment of employees into the co-op.

17. How is the state plan different from the federal plan?

The state plan has many fundamental differences from the Clinton proposal. A few examples of the differences are as follows:

Clinton: Health care reform can be fixed all at once with hundreds of complex, interrelated decisions made correctly.
State: Health care reform is a process that will require a sustained effort to ultimately reach the goal of affordable access.

Clinton: Access would be expanded immediately and financed by estimated savings.
State: Access would be expanded as actual savings are realized.

Clinton: A National Health Board would be created to regulate and enforce the national plan.
State: A Health Policy Commission would study important issues and make recommendations to the legislature.

Clinton: Costs would be contained through a global budget in the form of premium caps. The National Health Board would enforce these budgets, which will likely lead to rationing of care.
State: Costs would be contained by increasing the competitive forces in the market place.

Clinton: Employers would be mandated to provide coverage to their employees. This would likely lead to job losses in industries that cannot currently afford to buy coverage.
State: Individuals have a responsibility for their own coverage. Subsidies would eventually be enacted to help individuals receive coverage.

18. How will a federal health plan influence the state plan?

Until a federal health plan is approved, it is impossible to perceive the impact a federal plan would have on the state plan.

19. How will federal and state tax laws be changed to benefit the self-employed and individuals?

The legislature will be asked to approve a change in state tax laws to allow self-insured and individuals to deduct the full amount of health insurance premiums.

20. What will be the effect of expansion on the Medicaid budget?

It is anticipated that expansion of Medicaid will be largely funded through savings due to Medicaid capitation, Medicaid client cost sharing, and utilization of funds now available through the Utah Medical Assistance Program.

21. Will the expansion of Medicaid reduce the scope of services?

Reductions are not anticipated at this time.

22. What does capitation mean?

A method of payment for health services in which an individual or provider is paid a fixed dollar amount for each person served, regardless of the actual number or nature of services provided to each person in a set period of time, usually a year. Capitation is the characteristic payment method used in health maintenance organizations but is unusual for most private physicians' services.

23. What is a medical savings account?

Medical savings accounts (MSA) allow employers, self-employed individuals, and others to purchase a high deductible policy and put the premium cost differential into a medical savings account to pay for routine medical care. The funds in an MSA would belong to the insured and, if unspent, accumulate over time as savings to pre-fund future health care needs.

24. Will the plan affect the quality of health care?

There is sufficient consumer choice in the plan to safeguard the present quality of care in the health system.

PREPARED STATEMENT OF SENATOR GEORGE J. MITCHELL

Mr. Chairman, I commend you for holding this important hearing today to discuss the views of the Nation's governors on comprehensive health care reform. I want to welcome Governors Campbell, Dean, and Leavitt and extend a special welcome to our former colleague, Governor Chiles.

As a Senator from a small rural state, I believe that states must to have enough flexibility within a federal framework to design a health care system that will work for them. What will work in Southern California may not work in Maine. While managed competition may reduce health costs in a metropolitan area, managed collaboration—which would allow hospitals in rural areas to work together to avoid the costly duplication of services—may be the more successful delivery system in Maine. Both models may be used to improve the health care delivery system and benefit the consumer.

The public debate on health care reform has focused on the issues of cost and access. We know we can't keep doubling health care spending every five years.

As Governors, you are painfully aware of these costs. The cost of health care threatens the fiscal health of State governments across the nation.

The growth in the Medicaid program threatens states' ability to protect the most vulnerable, in our society, while at the same time forcing states to reduce or eliminate funding for other important services. Between 1988 and 1990, the average annual growth in Medicaid expenditures was 15.7 percent, and it is expected that state Medicaid spending will nearly triple between 1990 and 1995. Clearly this trend is unsustainable for both States and the federal government.

But we cannot control the costs of the Medicaid program without controlling overall health care spending.

Guaranteeing every American affordable private health insurance is equally important. Between 1991 and 1992, over two million Americans lost their health insurance coverage. Millions of others—in fact, nearly all Americans—fear losing their coverage if they become seriously ill or lose their job.

Coverage for affordable health care is a fundamental right in a Democratic society. But it is also a fundamental ingredient in achieving meaningful cost containment. For unless all Americans are in the system, cost shifting will continue.

We will never get control of health care spending if some are allowed to shift their share of the costs to others.

There are many points on which all Governors agree. But, there are other issues—difficult issues—on which there is no consensus. We face the same challenge in the Congress. Yet, we can all agree on the need for reform of the health care system. For to fail at this difficult task would be devastating for all states and for the nation. This will require compromise and it will require leadership—from you and from us. We cannot allow another Congress to pass without guaranteeing that every citizen of this nation has the same protection that we enjoy—affordable health care for ourselves and for our families.

PREPARED STATEMENT OF SENATOR DAVID PRYOR

Mr. Chairman, thank you for holding today's hearing. I appreciate the opportunity today to hear from governors who have been at the forefront of health reform. Judging from the work each of you have done in your state, I believe that you are well equipped to provide a wealth of information as we craft health reform legislation.

Almost two years ago, many of us here today, including Governors Chiles, attended a Finance hearing on state health care reform initiatives. With no hope for comprehensive health reform at the federal level, at that time we explored what could be done at the state level to achieve access to health care. I am pleased that we now have a President who is willing to go beyond just incremental change by making a commitment to passing legislation this year to assure health security for all Americans.

The President's plan recognizes the need for a strong state role in health reform, while establishing basic federal standards. I am pleased that the plan the President has put on the table goes far to relieve states of the hardships they now face. President Clinton's Health Security Act will help relieve states of the burden of Medicaid by incorporating the acute care portion of Medicaid into the new system. Also, the Clinton plan will help states to meet the long-term care needs of families. Having said that, I recognize that there are numerous implications for states in all of the plans before our Committee and I look forward to working with you on all of those issues.

States face escalating and unprecedented costs, ever-increasing numbers of uninsured, but most significantly the numerous personal tragedies that result from these problems.

I believe any effort we make must assist states in developing their own unique approaches to comprehensive health care reform for their citizens. As States will play a central role to implement health reform, state flexibility and an ability to innovate will be necessary to assure the success of any comprehensive plan.

In many areas of Arkansas, hospitals and doctors are nonexistent. And people lack the transportation to travel the many miles necessary to reach providers. Mr. Chairman, you and I know as well as anyone of that every state has its own unique problems. I would venture a guess that some of the problems faced by New Yorkers and Arkansans are about as different as night and day.

I was pleased to learn that recently a few members of your staff had the opportunity to visit the Arkansas Delta, including a school health clinic in Elaine and the Crittenden County Health Department in West Memphis.

As we work on health care reform legislation, it will be essential to ensure that the distinctive needs of all fifty states are met. Mr. Chairman, thank you again for holding this important hearing. We have an impressive group of witnesses, and I look forward to hearing their testimony.

○